Morning Gleanings

Handfuls of Wisdom Through

Daily Bible Reading

Word of His Mouth Publishers
Mooresboro, NC

All Scripture quotations are taken from the **King James Version** of the Bible.

ISBN: 978-1-941039-32-8
Printed in the United States of America
© 2023 Marc Smith

Word of His Mouth Publishers
Mooresboro, NC
www.wordofhismouth.com

PREFACE

I was born and raised in a Christian home, and from an early age, I have learned to follow the Lord in regard to giving, praying, and faithfully attending God's house as often as the doors were open. It was not until my early twenties that I began having any kind of daily devotion, but even with that, it was a mere cheesy five-minute daily devotional book with a single verse followed by an inspirational paragraph and/or quote. I married at age twenty-six and began to take notice of Sharla reading her Bible on a daily basis. I, too, began to read daily, howbeit just a handful of verses a day but reading through books of the Bible on a regular basis. It was not until early in my ministry, around 2006, that I began to read through the Bible cover to cover on a regular basis. One morning, I read in the book of **Matthew 26:40** *And he cometh unto the disciples, and findeth them asleep, and saith unto Peter, What, could ye not watch with me one hour?* One hour Jesus asked of His disciples, can you not watch and pray one hour? I have, since around 2008, given God the first hour of my day. On May 9, 2019, I began a daily devotional on social media called *Gleaning from this Mornings Reading.* I began to share simple thoughts and insights from my morning devotions. Just as Boaz instructed his servants to leave handfuls of blessings on the ground for Ruth to glean from, so did I want to share these thoughts and insights that God had given me through His Word and sharing as if it were just handfuls of God's Word to anyone who would listen. In the beginning, these devotionals were simply in written form. My daughter, Addison, suggested that I do a live devotion every morning along with the written devotion on social media. My wife, Sharla, suggested that I take these daily devotionals and put them into book format. Thank you to my wife and children for their inspiration and encouragement to turn these simple devotionals into a book.

Morning Gleanings is a collection of short, thought-provoking commentaries that can be used for daily devotions, individual Bible study, research, inspiration, or just casual everyday reading. My hope and prayer for each one who reads this book is to simply be inspired to allow God to speak to you through His Word. I pray that the simple short commentaries are a blessing and provoke you to study further. As you read through this book, hopefully and prayerfully, you, like I did, get just some handfuls of encouragement, inspiration, knowledge, and a blessing from studying God's Word.

Marc Smith
Senior Pastor,
Ambassador Baptist Church, Ennis, Texas

FOREWORD

Morning Gleanings is a terrific overview of thoughts and insight of verses throughout the Holy Bible from Genesis to Revelation, from someone who, in his own words was "drugged" as a kid; a phrase he takes from being "drug to Church" from his earliest memory by his parents every Sunday, Wednesday, and every special time the church doors were open. He was saved at the age of five years old in our home during a children's Bible program in Okinawa, Japan, with a missionary leading the children from Maranatha Baptist Church. From breakfast table devotions, along with his sister, his Dad, and his Mom, to sitting under seven different pastors as his dad's business career transferred the family fifteen times, living in four states, and two foreign countries, his Bible teaching came from the seven pastors. *Morning Gleanings* has taken him through the Bible many times over the past twenty plus years leading to the publishing of this book. I have known Brother Marc Smith from the day of his birth; yes, I am his proud dad and believe with all my heart you will find *Morning Gleanings* a tremendous help and encouragement to read and study your Bible daily. Today as Senior Pastor of Ambassador Baptist Church, Ennis, Texas, and author of *Mornings Gleanings,* he is also my pastor!

Dr. Don Smith
Pastor Emeritus, Ambassador Baptist Church, Ennis, TX
BEAMS Missionary
Bible Education and Missionary Service
Psalm 68:11

FOREWORD

Morning Gleanings. What a read! What a delight! My Brother Marc has read and given splendid insights of just how the Lord speaks to us as we read for "depth." Some like to read for distance, trying to just get through the Scriptures to show everyone we have read the whole council of God. I heard someone say to me years ago, "I want to hear God speak out loud!" I told them to read the Bible out loud. *Morning Gleanings* are just that, insights to the voice of God speaking to a pastor's heart through His Word. I am so thankful to have known Brother Marc and his family for many, many years. I have seen his growth as a husband, father, friend, and pastor who desires a walk with the Almighty God. I highly recommend this book and his approach as he gleans truths from the Word and the daily application which is so vital for a walk with the Lord. To God be the glory.

Dr. Bobby Bonner
Missionary/Evangelist/Associate Pastor
Founder & Visionary of International African Missions

GLEANINGS FROM THE BOOK OF GENESIS

Genesis 1:7 *And God made the firmament, and divided the waters which were under the firmament from the waters which were above the firmament: and it was so.*

"AND IT WAS SO"

There were six days of creation, and six times we read these four words. Six times God simply spoke, and six times it came to pass. There is no debate or question when God speaks. There is no one to challenge His Word. Know this, when God speaks, what He says will be!

———————————————————————————

Genesis 3:9 *And the LORD God called unto Adam, and said unto him, Where art thou?*

"WHERE ART THOU"

Adam and Eve were hiding in the trees because they had disobeyed God! Where art thou on this day? Are you trying to hide from God? Where do you stand with God today?

———————————————————————————

Genesis 11:4 *And they said, Go to, let us build us a city and a tower, whose top may reach unto heaven; and let us make us a name, lest we be scattered abroad upon the face of the whole earth.*

"AND LET US MAKE US A NAME"

There is a great danger in one's desire to make a name for himself. Pride goeth before destruction, and an haughty spirit before a fall. Our focus is to be on things eternal rather than that of this earth.

———————————————————————————

Genesis 13:10 *And Lot lifted up his eyes, and beheld all the plain of Jordan, that it was well watered every where, before the LORD destroyed Sodom and Gomorrah, even as the garden of the LORD, like the land of Egypt, as thou comest unto Zoar.*

"AND LOT LIFTED UP HIS EYES, AND BEHELD ALL THE PLAIN OF JORDAN"

The old saying, "The grass is not always greener on the other side of the fence," is never made more clear than in our text. The land was plush and green, flowing with pools and streams of water. It was greatly inhabited and good for business dealings. It seemed like a good opportunity for Lot and his family. Be careful, for what might seem right to the eyes of man is not always right in the eyes of God!

Genesis 13:12 *Abram dwelled in the land of Canaan, and Lot dwelled in the cities of the plain, and pitched his tent toward Sodom.*

"AND PITCHED HIS TENT TOWARD SODOM"

Be careful where you pitch your tent! Lot did not just set up his tent but rather faced the opening of his tent toward Sodom. Lot was enticed by all of Sodom's wickedness every morning as he awoke and stepped out of his tent. Eventually, Lot would give in to the flesh and move into the city of Sodom.

Genesis 13:14 *And the LORD said unto Abram, after that Lot was separated from him, Lift up now thine eyes, and look from the place where thou art northward, and southward, and eastward, and westward:*

"LIFT UP NOW THINE EYES"

Interesting, this account of Abraham. There was conflict with Pharaoh. There was conflict with Lot and his herdsman. There was conflict with the kings of the plain and Sodom and Gomorrah. There was conflict within his family between Sarah and Hagar, and yet, God said lift up now thine eyes. Too often, we allow circumstances to discourage us to the point that we lose our vision and fail to see that which God has promised.

Genesis 15:6 *And he believed in the LORD; and he counted it to him for righteousness.*

"AND HE BELIEVED IN THE LORD"

Many propose that Abraham was saved by works. I say nay but by faith, for Abraham believed the very Word of God as it was spoken to him in a vision. Abraham's faith in what God told him was counted unto him for righteousness. For by grace are ye saved through faith!

Genesis 18:14 *Is any thing too hard for the LORD? At the time appointed I will return unto thee, according to the time of life, and Sarah shall have a son.*

"IS ANY THING TOO HARD FOR THE LORD"

The very One who spoke the world into existence. Is anything too hard for Him? The very One who healed the sick and raised the dead. Is anything too hard for Him? The very One who was crucified, dead and buried, rose again on the third day, and now sits at the right hand of the Father. Is anything too hard for Him?

Genesis 19:16 *And while he lingered, the men laid hold upon his hand, and upon the hand of his wife, and upon the hand of his two daughters; the LORD being merciful unto him: and they brought him forth, and set him without the city.*

"AND WHILE HE LINGERED"

Many a Christian has stayed too long, whether it be in a position in life or in a place they should not have been to begin with. In Lot's case, it led to negligence, bad judgment, comprises, and led him to the brink of destruction! Though Lot is counted as a man of faith in

9

Hebrews 11, his poor judgment is reflected in his children who would become Moab and Ammon. What consequences await while you linger?

––––––––––––––––— ～ ——–––––––––––––––

Genesis 22:1 *And it came to pass after these things, that God did tempt Abraham, and said unto him, Abraham: and he said, Behold, here I am.*

"THAT GOD DID TEMPT ABRAHAM"

Nothing will test one's faith like that of a trial on a loved one. Even more so on a child. There is nothing more grievous than to sit helplessly while a young child suffers in a hospital bed. Thus Abraham's faith was tested through his only son Isaac. If God were to test your faith through one of your children how would your faith stand the test?

––––––––––––––––— ～ ——–––––––––––––––

Genesis 22:14 *And Abraham called the name of that place Jehovahjireh: as it is said to this day, In the mount of the LORD it shall be seen.*

"AND ABRAHAM CALLED THE NAME OF THAT PLACE JEHOVAHJIREH"

Jehovahjireh, or "The Lord will provide." Lord give us this day our daily bread. The just shall live by faith. What needs do you have today? The Lord knows what is best for you if we will just trust that He will provide that which we need!

––––––––––––––––— ～ ——–––––––––––––––

Genesis 24:48 *And I bowed down my head, and worshipped the LORD, and blessed the LORD God of my master Abraham, which had led me in the right way to take my master's brother's daughter unto his son.*

"WHICH HAD LED ME IN THE RIGHT WAY"

Abraham's servant gave God praise for a successful journey and mission! As we venture through this life, let us follow the leading of our Lord and Savior! Let us be led in the right way!

Genesis 26:35 *Which were a grief of mind unto Isaac and to Rebekah.*

"WHICH WERE A GRIEF OF MIND"

How important it is to marry with the approval of one's parents! Esau married two women of Hittite origin bringing with them their customs and unfamiliar ways. Neither Isaac nor Rebekah were very fond of them for they became grief to them both! This family feud would carry over into the next chapter as Rebekah fears that Jacob would make the same mistake!

Genesis 30:27 *And Laban said unto him, I pray thee, if I have found favour in thine eyes, tarry: for I have learned by experience that the LORD hath blessed me for thy sake.*

"FOR I HAVE LEARNED BY EXPERIENCE THAT THE LORD HATH BLESSED ME FOR THY SAKE"

Laban recognized that with Jacob around he gained and was better for it. Yes, though by trickery; but nonetheless, an acknowledgement of Jacob's well doing for Laban. It is a great lesson to learn in that we do not take for granted those who become a great blessing to us!

Genesis 32:25 *And when he saw that he prevailed not against him, he touched the hollow of his thigh; and the hollow of Jacob's thigh was out of joint, as he wrestled with him.*

"AND THE HOLLOW OF JACOB'S THIGH WAS OUT OF JOINT, AS HE WRESTLED WITH HIM"

Jacob wrestled with God all night. Jacob would wake the next morning with his hip out of joint. How is it that we think we can argue and fight against the will of God? For if we do, we will only go our way injured and limping. Sometimes an all-night wrestling match is just what we need to change our attitude. Jacob limped from that day forward, but spiritually, he was a changed man.

Genesis 34:1 *And Dinah the daughter of Leah, which she bare unto Jacob, went out to see the daughters of the land.*

NOTICE! She (Dinah) "WENT OUT TO SEE THE DAUGHTERS OF THE LAND"

Curiosity killed the cat! So the old saying goes! Dinah wanted to mix and mingle with the wrong crowd, which would lead to her being assaulted, kidnapped, her brothers committing murder to rescue her, and would lead her father Jacob to say these words in verse thirty "YE HAVE TROUBLED ME TO MAKE ME STINK AMONG THE INHABITANTS OF THE LAND." Our associations can lead to bad decisions!

Genesis 34:30 *And Jacob said to Simeon and Levi, Ye have troubled me to make me to stink among the inhabitants of the land, among the Canaanites and the Perizzites: and I being few in number, they shall gather themselves together against me, and slay me; and I shall be destroyed, I and my house.*

"YE HAVE TROUBLED ME TO MAKE ME TO STINK AMONG THE INHABITANTS OF THE LAND"

The actions of children have a far-reaching effect beyond their own selfish desires. Dinah, Jacob's daughter, "went out to see the daughters of the land." By stepping out from under the protection of her family, she was kidnapped and assaulted. Her brothers then took revenge and killed her assailants. Jacob's response is that his children's actions have given him a bad reputation. Your actions have a far greater reach than what you might think!

Genesis 35:18 *And it came to pass, as her soul was in departing, (for she died) that she called his name Benoni: but his father called him Benjamin.*

"SHE CALLED HIS NAME BENONI. BUT HIS FATHER CALLED HIM BENJAMIN"

Before Rachel died, she named her son Benoni, but Jacob named him Benjamin. We see pictures of Christ all throughout scripture and yet here another. Benoni means "Son of my sorrow." Benjamin means "Son of my right hand." I am reminded of the words of **Isaiah 53:3** *He is despised and rejected of men; a man of sorrows*...and yet now He sits at the right hand of the Father in Heaven!

Genesis 39:2 *And the LORD was with Joseph, and he was a prosperous man; and he was in the house of his master the Egyptian.*

"AND THE LORD WAS WITH JOSEPH, AND HE WAS A PROSPEROUS MAN"

"I will never leave thee nor forsake thee" is a promise from the Lord to His people. Though Joseph went through many a trial and hardship, he remained faithful and pure. He was a prosperous man in that he excelled in all that he did. Likewise, we can do all things through Christ who gives us strength!

13

Genesis 39:3 *And his master saw that the LORD was with him, and that the LORD made all that he did to prosper in his hand.*

"AND HIS MASTER SAW THAT THE LORD WAS WITH HIM"

Man looketh upon the outward appearance but God sees the heart! What is in the heart will be revealed outwardly in one's appearance and his actions! Actions sometimes speak louder than words. Joseph's master saw the Lord working in and through Joseph in all that he did. The Lord blessed Joseph in that all that Joseph did prospered!

Genesis 41:38 *And Pharaoh said unto his servants, Can we find such a one as this is, a man in whom the Spirit of God is?*

"CAN WE FIND SUCH A ONE AS THIS IS, A MAN IN WHOM THE SPIRIT OF GOD IS?"

Would to God there were Christians like Joseph who stood out from the rest! The greatest compliment a Christian can receive from the world is that they see something different in us! MAY THEY SEE IN ME, A MAN IN WHOM THE SPIRIT OF GOD IS!

Genesis 42:18 *And Joseph said unto them the third day, This do, and live; for I fear God:*

"FOR I FEAR GOD"

Joseph has but one testimony in all that he has experienced. Sold into slavery, falsely accused, imprisoned and forgotten and yet he has never faltered in trusting God. How quickly do we lose faith in our times of trial. No matter the situation, let us, like Joseph, fear God.

Genesis 45:24 *So he sent his brethren away, and they departed: and he said unto them, See that ye fall not out by the way.*

"SEE THAT YE FALL NOT OUT BY THE WAY"

Joseph had forgiven his brothers, for God had truly blessed in spite of all that his brothers had done to him. Joseph encourages his brothers to not quarrel and accuse one another. Often, we beat ourselves up over past mistakes when indeed God can use our failures to His honor and glory if we will let HIM!

Genesis 48:11 *And Israel said unto Joseph, I had not thought to see thy face: and, lo, God hath shewed me also thy seed.*

"AND, LO, GOD HATH SHEWED ME ALSO THY SEED"

The joy of a father is to not only live to see their children grow up but to see them likewise become fathers of children. The job of a parent is not to raise children to keep them at home but to train them up in the way that they should go, so they are equipped with the tools of knowledge to one day raise families of their own!

Genesis 50:19 *And Joseph said unto them, Fear not: for am I in the place of God?*

"FOR AM I IN THE PLACE OF GOD"

Many times we question God's timing in our lives, and yet the just shall live by faith. Learning to trust can be a difficult thing to do especially in difficult times. Joseph answers the apology from his brothers for the hardships they put him through with true wisdom. His view was that he was right where God wanted him to be!

GLEANINGS FROM THE BOOK OF EXODUS

Exodus 3:7 *And the LORD said, I have surely seen the affliction of my people which are in Egypt, and have heard their cry by reason of their taskmasters; for I know their sorrows;*

"FOR I KNOW THEIR SORROWS"

God saw the affliction of the children of Israel. He heard their cry and complaint of affliction. He was aware of their sorrows. God is not blind to our hurts, pains, afflictions, and sorrows. He sees all, and He knows all. A child's cry will not go unnoticed by the Father!

Exodus 4:11 *And the LORD said unto him, Who hath made man's mouth? or who maketh the dumb, or deaf, or the seeing, or the blind? have not I the LORD?*

"WHO HATH MADE MAN'S MOUTH"

We often give excuses for why we can't serve based upon our physical ability, and yet we forget that God is the one who allowed that physical disability to come into our lives. God used Moses even with his speech impediment to lead His people out of Egypt.

Exodus 6:3 *And I appeared unto Abraham, unto Isaac, and unto Jacob, by the name of God Almighty, but by my name JEHOVAH was I not known to them.*

"BUT BY MY NAME JEHOVAH WAS I NOT KNOWN TO THEM"

Previously, God had made himself known to Abraham, Isaac, and Jacob as El Shaddai, or put another way, "God Almighty," for He is able to do and perform the impossible. But now He would be known to them as JEHOVAH, and the children of Israel would now see those promises manifested with great strength and power from almighty God!

Exodus 6:5 *And I have also heard the groaning of the children of Israel, whom the Egyptians keep in bondage; and I have remembered my covenant.*

"AND I HAVE REMEMBERED MY COVENANT"

God had not forgotten His promise to Abraham in that out of Abraham's seed would come a great nation. God heard the cries of Israel and remembered His promise! God's promises are true and faithful. Every promise He has given us He can and will fulfill. I assure you, the Lord has not forgotten His children!

Exodus 9:14 *For I will at this time send all my plagues upon thine heart, and upon thy servants, and upon thy people; that thou mayest know that there is none like me in all the earth.*

"THAT THOU MAYEST KNOW THAT THERE IS NONE LIKE ME IN ALL THE EARTH"

The magicians of Egypt could mimic a few of the plagues but only mimic them, for they could not reproduce them in such capacity as God had done. There is no greater power on Earth or in Heaven that can compare to the mighty hand of God.

Exodus 10:3 *And Moses and Aaron came in unto Pharaoh, and said unto him, Thus saith the LORD God of the Hebrews, How long wilt thou refuse to humble thyself before me? let my people go, that they may serve me.*

"HOW LONG WILT THOU REFUSE TO HUMBLE THYSELF BEFORE ME"

What a great question. Is your pride hindering you from obeying the Lord's command? What will it take for you to humble yourself and obey? It cost Pharaoh everything. What will it cost you?

Exodus 12:11 And thus shall ye eat it; with your loins girded, your shoes on your feet, and your staff in your hand; and ye shall eat it in haste: it is the LORD'S passover.

"WITH YOUR LOINS GIRDED, YOUR SHOES ON YOUR FEET, AND YOUR STAFF IN YOUR HAND"

The children of Israel had been in bondage for over four hundred years. The time had come for God to deliver the children of Israel. Moses' direction was for them to be ready to move at a moment's notice, for God was going to act on their behalf! Many times we as Christians pray for God to do something, and yet we make no preparations ourselves to move when God does. If you expect God to move, then be prepared when He does!

Exodus 14:13 And Moses said unto the people, Fear ye not, stand still, and see the salvation of the LORD, which he will shew to you to day: for the Egyptians whom ye have seen to day, ye shall see them again no more for ever.

"FEAR YE NOT, STAND STILL, AND SEE THE SALVATION OF THE LORD"

With the Red Sea on one side and the Egyptian army on the other, the Israelites find themselves with no solution and no answers to their predicament. There are times in our lives when we find ourselves in situations where there seems to be no answer or solution. It is in these times God wants to reveal His glory. We have only but to fear not and stand still.

Exodus 14:15 *And the LORD said unto Moses, Wherefore criest thou unto me? speak unto the children of Israel, that they go forward:*

"SPEAK UNTO THE CHILDREN OF ISRAEL, THAT THEY GO FORWARD"

The time spent complaining would be better spent moving forward. Too many times we want to sit and wallow in self-pity. Our prayer time is often spent in despair and of heavy heart. The Lord declared to the children of Israel, "Why cry unto me? Get up and move forward!"

Exodus 19:5 *Now therefore, if ye will obey my voice indeed, and keep my covenant, then ye shall be a peculiar treasure unto me above all people: for all the earth is mine:*

"YE SHALL BE A PECULIAR TREASURE UNTO ME"

The word peculiar means "precious." In the world of antiquities, the better shape something is in, the more valuable it becomes! God said that if we will take care of ourselves spiritually that we would be a PRECIOUS TREASURE to Him above all people! Do we care more about what the world thinks? On the other hand, do we care more about what God thinks?

Exodus 23:7 *Keep thee far from a false matter; and the innocent and righteous slay thou not: for I will not justify the wicked.*

"KEEP THEE FAR FROM A FALSE MATTER"

The gossip of a child of God is not unheard of. Many a Pastor has huddled in corners and falsely accused another. We are to abstain from any false matter whether great or small. To falsely accuse another is to bring to light the true character of oneself. A child of God would be wise to stay away from such matters.

Exodus 23:25 *And ye shall serve the LORD your God, and he shall bless thy bread, and thy water; and I will take sickness away from the midst of thee.*

"AND HE SHALL BLESS THY BREAD"

It really is very simple in that those who serve the LORD God shall be blessed both in provision and in health. Could it be that those who will not serve the LORD are subjecting themselves to poverty and sickness?

Exodus 24:10 *And they saw the God of Israel: and there was under his feet as it were a paved work of a sapphire stone, and as it were the body of heaven in his clearness.*

"AND THEY SAW THE GOD OF ISRAEL"

The elders of Israel were given just a glimpse of His glory! The feet of God Almighty! A sapphire stone for His footstool! Many a Christian would desire to see His face as Moses did. We would be overcome with worship and adoration at just a glimpse of His feet!

Exodus 28:30 *And thou shalt put in the breastplate of judgment the Urim and the Thummim; and they shall be upon Aaron's heart, when he goeth in before the LORD: and Aaron shall bear the judgment of the children of Israel upon his heart before the LORD continually.*

"AND AARON SHALL BEAR THE JUDGMENT OF THE CHILDREN OF ISRAEL UPON HIS HEART BEFORE THE LORD CONTINUALLY"

Aaron was to keep the Urim and Thummim close to his heart continually. Urim means "light," and Thummim means "perfect truth." Did not the Psalmist say, "Thy word is a lamp unto my feet, and a light unto my path"? And do not we read, "Thy word have I hid in mine heart, that I might not sin against thee"?

Exodus 28:36 *And thou shalt make a plate of pure gold, and grave upon it, like the engravings of a signet, HOLINESS TO THE LORD.*

"HOLINESS TO THE LORD"

The headdress for the priest had a signet on it that read "HOLINESS TO THE LORD," a declaration to all he encountered that he was committed to a life of holiness unto the Lord. When people see you, what is declared in your life? Is it holiness?

Exodus 32:8 *They have turned aside quickly out of the way which I commanded them: they have made them a molten calf, and have worshipped it, and have sacrificed thereunto, and said, These be thy gods, O Israel, which have brought thee up out of the land of Egypt.*

"THEY HAVE TURNED ASIDE QUICKLY OUT OF THE WAY WHICH I COMMANDED THEM"

How quickly a child of God can fall into sin. We should stay focused on what God would have us to do and not let or allow discouragement, trials, and tribulations to detour us away from God's plan. God had commanded them and given them direction, and yet how quickly they went a different way!

Exodus 32:24 *And I said unto them, Whosoever hath any gold, let them break it off. So they gave it me: then I cast it into the fire, and there came out this calf.*

"AND THERE CAME OUT THIS CALF"

The proclamation that Aaron threw gold in the fire and a golden calf just appeared is absurd. The excuse given for Aaron's actions is almost humorous, and yet the excuse is given nonetheless. It is easy for us to be critical of Aaron, and yet we give many an absurd excuse for not serving the Lord. That proverbial calf in our lives did not just appear by chance.

Exodus 32:26 *Then Moses stood in the gate of the camp, and said, Who is on the LORD'S side? let him come unto me. And all the sons of Levi gathered themselves together unto him.*

"WHO IS ON THE LORD'S SIDE"

Interesting, this statement is! For Moses was not addressing a heathen congregation but rather a backslidden nation of Israel. God's chosen people! That same cry ought to be shouted from our pulpits even today! A challenge to those who claim to be Christians. Who is on the Lord's side? Step forward and be counted! Interesting that those who chose to be on the Lord's side stood out from the rest.

Exodus 33:14 *And he said, My presence shall go with thee, and I will give thee rest.*

"MY PRESENCE SHALL GO WITH THEE, AND I WILL GIVE THEE REST"

Though I walk through the valley of the shadow of death, I will fear no evil! Walking with God and knowing His will gives the Christian confidence that no matter what may come, we may find rest and have peace in knowing that God is in control!

Exodus 35:30 *And Moses said unto the children of Israel, See, the LORD hath called by name Bezaleel the son of Uri, the son of Hur, of the tribe of Judah;* **31** *And he hath filled him with the spirit of God, in wisdom, in understanding, and in knowledge, and in all manner of workmanship;* **32** *And to devise curious works, to work in gold, and in silver, and in brass,* **33** *And in the cutting of stones, to set them, and in carving of wood, to make any manner of cunning work.*

"TO MAKE ANY MANNER OF CUNNING WORK"

I was reminded as I read this portion of scripture that ministers of the gospel are not the only ones that are to be spirit-filled! Notice verse thirty-one: *"And he hath filled him with the spirit of God, in wisdom, in understanding, and in knowledge, and in all manner of workmanship..."* No matter what line of work you are in, if you are a child of God, then be your best! In all manner of workmanship!

Exodus 39:30 *And they made the plate of the holy crown of pure gold, and wrote upon it a writing, like to the engravings of a signet, HOLINESS TO THE LORD.*

"HOLINESS TO THE LORD"

A constant reminder to the high priest of his mission. It was to be worn on his head for all to see. His oath was to do all things in a manner of holiness unto the Lord. This was not only a reminder to himself but a testimony to others about him of his position. Likewise, let us remember that as children of God, we also wear a signet of Salvation. Let us act accordingly, doing all things as unto holiness unto the Lord, for others are watching!

GLEANINGS FROM THE BOOK OF LEVITICUS

Leviticus 6:13 *The fire shall ever be burning upon the altar; it shall never go out.*

"IT SHALL NEVER GO OUT"

It could be the most important of jobs concerning the priesthood. For without the fire, the sacrifices would not be made. It was important that the fire not go out. Likewise, in our daily walk as Christians, it is important that our fire not go out and that we remain faithful and committed to sharing the gospel with those around us. As the old hymn says, "We'll work till Jesus comes!" Let us keep the fire of service burning until we see Christ!

Leviticus 10:1 *And Nadab and Abihu, the sons of Aaron, took either of them his censer, and put fire therein, and put incense thereon, and offered strange fire before the LORD, which he commanded them not.*

"AND OFFERED STRANGE FIRE BEFORE THE LORD"

As I read this story about Nadab and Abihu (who, after being given specific instructions on how to prepare a sacrifice, offered up strange fire unto the Lord), I could not help but wonder how many preachers stand behind the pulpits of America and proclaim things that are considered strange to our Lord!

Leviticus 10:19 *And Aaron said unto Moses, Behold, this day have they offered their sin offering and their burnt offering before the LORD; and such things have befallen me: and if I had eaten the sin offering to day, should it have been accepted in the sight of the LORD?*

"AND SUCH THINGS HAVE BEFALLEN ME"

Aaron was commanded to eat of the sin offering and the blood poured out upon the altar. Moses noticed the incomplete work of

Aaron and rebuked him for it. Aaron's response is very interesting, for he said he could not in the midst of his sorrow over the loss of his two sons. It is to be a joyful thing to know that God has forgiven our sins, but how can we rejoice while wallowing in self-pity? There is a time to mourn, but then let us wash and rise up, for there is a God to be praised!

Leviticus 15:2 *Speak unto the children of Israel, and say unto them, When any man hath a running issue out of his flesh, because of his issue he is unclean.*

"BECAUSE OF HIS ISSUE HE IS UNCLEAN"

To everything physical, there is a spiritual. The Levitical laws were in place not just for law and order. There is a call for cleanliness. One who practices cleanliness tends to be healthier and therefore sets the example for spiritual purity. The people could not bring a sacrifice to the temple if they were physically unclean. In like manner we also should come into His presence clean spiritually.

Leviticus 17:7 *And they shall no more offer their sacrifices unto devils, after whom they have gone a whoring. This shall be a statute forever unto them throughout their generations.*

"AND THEY SHALL NO MORE OFFER THEIR SACRIFICES UNTO DEVILS"

Many of the children of Israel had taken on Egyptian customs and mannerisms. God demanded a change. A true child of God must put away the old way of life and walk in the newness of life. Man cannot serve two masters. He must choose, and so must we as Christians. Though we claim to be a child of God, we tend to carry with us worldly habits. Choose you this day whom ye will serve!

Leviticus 18:4 *Ye shall do my judgments, and keep mine ordinances, to walk therein: I am the LORD your God.*

"I AM THE LORD YOUR GOD"

All throughout the book of Leviticus, God calls for His chosen people to separate themselves from uncleanliness! He tells them to not take on the traditions and mannerisms of other nations. He clearly proclaims throughout Leviticus, "I am the Lord YOUR GOD!" Is He your God? If He is, then why do you not do His judgments and keep His ordinances? Many declare Him their God, but their actions say different!

Leviticus19:28 *Ye shall not make any cuttings in your flesh for the dead, nor print any marks upon you: I am the LORD.*

"YE SHALL NOT MAKE ANY CUTTINGS IN YOUR FLESH FOR THE DEAD"

The acts of self-mutilation and tattooing images of idols on one's flesh were widely practiced throughout various cultures. These practices were implemented often over the death of a loved one. These acts are forbidden, for our God represents the living. To do such acts is to reverence the dead.

Leviticus 21:5 *They shall not make baldness upon their head, neither shall they shave off the corner of their beard, nor make any cuttings in their flesh.* **6.** *They shall be holy unto their God, and not profane the name of their God: for the offerings of the LORD made by fire, and the bread of their God, they do offer: therefore they shall be holy.*

"THEY SHALL BE HOLY UNTO THEIR GOD"

Interesting that before this statement, God instructs them not to take on the ways of the heathen in their appearance! How we present ourselves is a reflection of HIS holiness in our lives!

Leviticus 24:4 *He shall order the lamps upon the pure candlestick before the LORD continually.*

"BEFORE THE LORD CONTINUALLY"

The children of Israel were asked to bring and give willingly olive oil to be used in the burning of the candlestick in the tabernacle so that the light would not go out before the Lord. It is not just the man of God's responsibility to keep the light burning. All who call Him Lord must play a part in sharing the light of Jesus Christ! As He is light, let us also walk in that light!

Leviticus 26:14 *But if ye will not hearken unto me, and will not do all these commandments;* **15** *And if ye shall despise my statutes, or if your soul abhor my judgments, so that ye will not do all my commandments, but that ye break my covenant:* **16** *I also will do this unto you; I will even appoint over you terror, consumption, and the burning ague, that shall consume the eyes, and cause sorrow of heart: and ye shall sow your seed in vain, for your enemies shall eat it.*

"BUT IF YE WILL NOT HEARKEN UNTO ME"

The Levitical law is a call to purity both in the priesthood and the partaker of sacrifice and service. God declares to the children of Israel that if they did not approach the Tabernacle in purity and ignored God's command, then they as a people would suffer the consequences. Likewise the nation that refuses to acknowledge and obey God's commands are subject to the consequences. Is it any wonder the United States of America has the problems that she has?

Leviticus 26:44 *And yet for all that, when they be in the land of their enemies, I will not cast them away, neither will I abhor them, to destroy them utterly, and to break my covenant with them: for I am the LORD their God.*

"AND YET FOR ALL THAT, WHEN THEY BE IN THE LAND OF THEIR ENEMIES, I WILL NOT CAST THEM AWAY"

Chapter twenty-six details the horrible plagues and tribulations that God would bring upon the children of Israel if they did not follow His statutes and obey His commands. Yet His promise to make them a great nation would still stand. Praise the Lord He does not just throw us away when we fail Him!

Leviticus 27:1 *And the LORD spake unto Moses, saying,*

"AND THE LORD SPAKE UNTO MOSES"

I counted this morning at least thirty-six times or more in Leviticus this phrase, "AND THE LORD SPAKE UNTO MOSES!" How many of us who claim to be Christians actually took the time to speak to God this morning, and how many can say that God spoke to them?

GLEANINGS FROM THE BOOK OF NUMBERS

Numbers 4:18 *Cut ye not off the tribe of the families of the Kohathites from among the Levites:* **19** *But thus do unto them, that they may live, and not die, when they approach unto the most holy things: Aaron and his sons shall go in, and appoint them every one to his service and to his burden:*

"BUT THUS DO UNTO THEM, THAT THEY MAY LIVE, AND NOT DIE"

The Kohathites, of all the families of the Levites, were given the responsibility of moving the most holy of items in the tabernacle. God tells Moses and Aaron to take great care in giving instructions as to how to handle the ark; for, if handled wrong, it would cost them their life! King David failed to give such instruction when he moved the ark on a Philistine cart. The ox stumbled, and Uzzah reached up to steady the ark and was killed. When it comes to God's Word, it is of most importance how it is presented. It is a matter of life and death, Heaven or Hell, lost or saved!

Numbers 5:29 *This is the law of jealousies, when a wife goeth aside to another instead of her husband, and is defiled;*

"THIS IS THE LAW OF JEALOUSIES"

One of the most misunderstood chapters in all of scripture is found here in Numbers. Often this chapter is used to justify abortion; however, nowhere in this passage is it said that she is with child. The key to understanding this text is in one statement. This is the law of jealousies. It is the husband that is jealous, not the wife. God is a jealous God, and He is jealous for us.

Numbers 9:8 *And Moses said unto them, Stand still, and I will hear what the LORD will command concerning you.*

"STAND STILL"

A certain number of men approached Moses about a circumstance beyond their control! Leading into Passover, they had an unfortunate death. They were not to touch anything dead and keep the Passover. When circumstances beyond our control find their way into our lives and leave us feeling unsure, it would do us well to just stand still and wait on the Lord!

Numbers 9:23 *At the commandment of the LORD they rested in the tents, and at the commandment of the LORD they journeyed: they kept the charge of the LORD, at the commandment of the LORD by the hand of Moses.*

"AT THE COMMANDMENT OF THE LORD"

They rested at God's command!
They moved forward at God's command!
They kept the charge (order) (responsibilities) at God's command!
In all that we do, may it be of God!

Numbers 11:1 *And when the people complained, it displeased the LORD: and the LORD heard it; and his anger was kindled; and the fire of the LORD burnt among them, and consumed them that were in the uttermost parts of the camp.*

"AND WHEN THE PEOPLE COMPLAINED, IT DISPLEASED THE LORD"

A complaining Christian is one who displeases the Lord! Let us be content in the service that God has put us in!

Numbers 11:4 *And the mixt multitude that was among them fell a lusting: and the children of Israel also wept again, and said, Who shall give us flesh to eat?*

"AND THE MIXT MULTITUDE THAT WAS AMONG THEM FELL A LUSTING"

There were Egyptian natives who left and fled with the children of Israel when they fled Egypt. These same people are complaining and trying to convince God's people that life was better in Egypt. A word of caution in that we be careful of friendships made with unbelievers, for they may desire to draw you away from what is God's plan!

Numbers 11:23 *And the LORD said unto Moses, Is the LORD'S hand waxed short? Thou shalt see now whether my word shall come to pass unto thee or not.*

"AND THE LORD SAID UNTO MOSES, IS THE LORD'S HAND WAXED SHORT"

God asks Moses a question. Is the LORD'S hand waxed short? Put another way, is the LORD'S hand limited? How often do we limit God through our doubts and complaining? Let us acknowledge Him for who He is and that there is nothing our God cannot do!

Numbers 14:9 *Only rebel not ye against the LORD, neither fear ye the people of the land; for they are bread for us: their defence is departed from them, and the LORD is with us: fear them not.*

"ONLY REBEL NOT YE AGAINST THE LORD"

God had promised the children of Israel a land flowing with milk and honey, but the people did not trust the Lord to give it to them. Joshua and Caleb begged the children of Israel to not rebel against the Lord. To fear man and not trust the Lord is rebellion. How often do we miss what God has in store for us due to our rebellion?

Numbers 16:5 *And he spake unto Korah and unto all his company, saying, Even to morrow the LORD will shew who are his, and who is holy; and will cause him to come near unto him: even him whom he hath chosen will he cause to come near unto him.*

"EVEN TO MORROW THE LORD WILL SHEW WHO ARE HIS, AND WHO IS HOLY"

Korah had gathered two hundred fifty men together in an attempt to overthrow Moses. Moses accepted the challenge, and God separated the evil followers of Korah from the Godliness of Moses. Those that followed Korah were consumed by fire. There is coming a day when God will again separate the holy from evil, and they too will be burned with fire. The fires of HELL!

Numbers 16:48 *And he stood between the dead and the living; and the plague was stayed.*

"AND HE STOOD BETWEEN THE DEAD AND THE LIVING"

After God consumed Korah and his followers, the people began to murmur and accuse Moses of murder. God brought a great plague upon the people that killed fourteen thousand seven hundred people. The Bible says that Moses stood between the living and the dead. What a great picture of our Savior. He is the difference between life and death.

Numbers 19:12 *He shall purify himself with it on the third day, and on the seventh day he shall be clean: but if he purify not himself the third day, then the seventh day he shall not be clean.*

"HE SHALL PURIFY HIMSELF WITH IT ON THE THIRD DAY"

This is a prophetic verse in regards to the sanctification of the Christian in comparison to the cleanliness of the high priest. If the priest were to touch a dead body, he was to separate himself from the congregation for seven days. He was to wash himself both on the third day and on the seventh. Prophetic how? The wages of sin is death, and yet on the third day, Christ conquered death and rose from the dead that we might grow in grace over time spiritually!

Numbers 20:5 *And wherefore have ye made us to come up out of Egypt, to bring us in unto this evil place? it is no place of seed, or of figs, or of vines, or of pomegranates; neither is there any water to drink.*

"AND WHEREFORE HAVE YE MADE US TO COME UP OUT OF EGYPT TO BRING US IN UNTO THIS EVIL PLACE"

God had delivered His people out of Egypt and was taking them into a land flowing with milk and honey. The people murmured and called the place God had them in an evil place. Let us always keep our eyes on the finish line, for it is in the middle of the race we seem the weariest. If it is part of God's plan, then no matter how rough the journey, He will carry us through!

Numbers 20:12 *And the LORD spake unto Moses and Aaron, Because ye believed me not, to sanctify me in the eyes of the children of Israel, therefore ye shall not bring this congregation into the land which I have given them.*

"BECAUSE YE BELIEVED ME NOT"

Moses had been instructed to simply speak to the rock, and it would bring forth water, yet he struck the rock not once but twice in anger! Our way often is the hard way, and yet in our stubbornness, we push forward instead of just allowing God to move for us!

Numbers 20:17 *Let us pass, I pray thee, through thy country: we will not pass through the fields, or through the vineyards, neither will we drink of the water of the wells: we will go by the king's high way, we will not turn to the right hand nor to the left, until we have passed thy borders.*

"WE WILL GO BY THE KING'S HIGH WAY, WE WILL NOT TURN TO THE RIGHT HAND NOR TO THE LEFT"

The king's highway was a wider road than most, mainly used for great caravans and armies! Moses had promised the king of Edom that they would not venture into private lands but would simply pass through the land on the king's highway!
Likewise, we are just passing through! Let us stay true to the KING OF KINGS' highway, turning to neither the right nor the left until we reach Heaven's borders!

Numbers 22:18 *And Balaam answered and said unto the servants of Balak, If Balak would give me his house full of silver and gold, I cannot go beyond the word of the LORD my God, to do less or more.*

"I CANNOT GO BEYOND THE WORD OF THE LORD MY GOD TO DO LESS OR MORE"

For what is it to a man if he gain the whole world but lose his own soul? Balaam said, "I cannot do less or more than what the Lord requires of me to do." Likewise, we should have that same heart in us. The desire of a child of God's heart should be to serve the Lord, not the riches the world has to offer.

Numbers 23:21 *He hath not beheld iniquity in Jacob, neither hath he seen perverseness in Israel: the LORD his God is with him, and the shout of a king is among them.*

"AND THE SHOUT OF A KING IS AMONG THEM"

Balaam was to curse the children of Israel on behalf of Balak. As when God rebuked Peter for not eating what Peter deemed unclean (God asked Peter why he would call something unclean that God calls clean), likewise, how can Balaam curse a people whom God has blessed? There is a shout of a King among them. The KING OF KINGS AND LORD OF LORDS!

Numbers 24:13 *If Balak would give me his house full of silver and gold, I cannot go beyond the commandment of the LORD, to do either good or bad of mine own mind; but what the LORD saith, that will I speak?*

"I CANNOT GO BEYOND THE COMMANDMENT OF THE LORD"

Many a man of God has sought out a pulpit based upon the paycheck! Moreover, many a message has been swayed due to the wealth sitting in a pew! Let us not be swayed by silver and gold but rather be obedient to the Lord's command!

Numbers 25:1 *And Israel abode in Shittim, and the people began to commit whoredom with the daughters of Moab.*

"AND ISRAEL ABODE IN SHITTIM"

Israel ventured into the land of Moab and stayed. The children of Israel began to take part in their ritualistic pagan practices. Lot did the same thing, for he pitched his tent toward Sodom and eventually took up residence in Sodom. Be careful where you abide, for it is there that you will remain.

Numbers 27:12 *And the LORD said unto Moses, Get thee up into this mount Abarim, and see the land which I have given unto the children of Israel.*

"AND SEE THE LAND WHICH I HAVE GIVEN UNTO THE CHILDREN OF ISRAEL"

Reading the passage, I cannot help but think that though Moses was not going to enter the promise land, God yet gave him a vision of days to come from atop Mount Pisgah. Though we cannot see the future, sometimes a little alone time with God helps us rise above the day's current events, and God through His word gives us a hope for tomorrow!

Numbers 30:2 *If a man vow a vow unto the LORD, or swear an oath to bind his soul with a bond; he shall not break his word, he shall do according to all that proceedeth out of his mouth.*

"IF A MAN VOW A VOW UNTO THE LORD...HE SHALL NOT BREAK HIS WORD"

One should not be so careless with his promises. God cannot lie and so are His promises true. Likewise, God expects His children to fulfill their promises. To vow a vow and not fulfill that vow is nothing more than a lie. Satan is the father of lies! Therefore, let us be careful not to make a promise we cannot keep!

Numbers 32:23 *But if ye will not do so, behold, ye have sinned against the LORD: and be sure your sin will find you out.*

"AND BE SURE YOUR SIN WILL FIND YOU OUT"

A truth so many ignore. When we deliberately sin against the Lord, it will not go unnoticed! The Lord will hold you accountable for your actions. It may take days, months or even years, but be assured your sin will come back to you and be held to your account!

Numbers 33:55 *But if ye will not drive out the inhabitants of the land from before you; then it shall come to pass, that those which ye let remain of them shall be pricks in your eyes, and thorns in your sides, and shall vex you in the land wherein ye dwell.*

"THAT THOSE WHICH YE LET REMAIN OF THEM SHALL BE PRICKS IN YOUR EYES, AND THORNS IN YOUR SIDES"

The children of Israel were instructed to drive out completely the inhabitants of the land. A failure to do so would result in hardships down the road! A good lesson to learn! Let us do things right the first time! In ministry, I try to apply this rule! DO IT RIGHT, DO IT WELL, DO IT ONCE! Sometimes it is necessary to revisit things that are understood. When it comes to God's commands, obedience will save us much heartache down the road!

Numbers 35:30 *Whoso killeth any person, the murderer shall be put to death by the mouth of witnesses: but one witness shall not testify against any person to cause him to die.*

"THE MURDERER SHALL BE PUT TO DEATH BY THE MOUTH OF WITNESSES"

The act of heresay is a dangerous thing, even to the end of taking one's life needlessly. Notice the accusations against one who commits murder must be by more than just one accuser. An accusation by one is just simply that, but an accusation by two or more, then an individual could be found guilty.

GLEANINGS FROM THE BOOK OF DEUTERONOMY

Deuteronomy 1:17 *Ye shall not respect persons in judgment; but ye shall hear the small as well as the great; ye shall not be afraid of the face of man; for the judgment is God's: and the cause that is too hard for you, bring it unto me, and I will hear it.*

"YE SHALL NOT BE AFRAID OF THE FACE OF MAN; FOR THE JUDGEMENT IS GODS"

It is not for a man to pass judgment based on his personal feelings and desires, for God is no respecter of persons and therefore neither should we be. If God has given you a position of authority, then lead and judge in a Godly manner!

Deuteronomy 1:30 *The LORD your God which goeth before you, he shall fight for you, according to all that he did for you in Egypt before your eyes;*

"HE SHALL FIGHT FOR YOU"

If God is for us, who can be against us? If God has called you to go, then He will go before you and fight for you! I assure you there will be obstacles, trials, and tribulations, but we will not face them alone, for HE SHALL FIGHT FOR YOU!

Deuteronomy 2:5 *Meddle not with them; for I will not give you of their land, no, not so much as a foot breadth; because I have given mount Seir unto Esau for a possession.*

"MEDDLE NOT WITH THEM"

Many a child of God has created more trouble for themselves by taking part in things they would do well to leave alone. Busybodies giving input where it is not needed. Trying to fix that which is not broken. The proverbial turning of a mole hill into a mountain. In other words...mind your own business.

Deuteronomy 3:24 *O Lord GOD, thou hast begun to shew thy servant thy greatness, and thy mighty hand: for what God is there in heaven or in earth, that can do according to thy works, and according to thy might?*

"FOR WHAT GOD IS THERE IN HEAVEN OR IN EARTH, THAT CAN DO ACCORDING TO THY WORKS, AND ACCORDING TO THY MIGHT"

God had proven Himself over and over again to the children of Israel, yet they feared the coming battles they would face to occupy the Promised Land. How quickly we forget the goodness of our God and let fear creep into our daily lives.

Deuteronomy 4:9 *Only take heed to thyself, and keep thy soul diligently, lest thou forget the things which thine eyes have seen, and lest they depart from thy heart all the days of thy life: but teach them thy sons, and thy sons' sons;*

"AND KEEP THY SOUL DILIGENTLY, LEST THOU FORGET THE THINGS WHICH THINE EYES HAVE SEEN"

A warning from God against idolatry. God warns that they should not forget what they have seen and heard, for the souls of future generations are depending on it. We have a duty to teach and train up future generations to know and worship this very same God. Our children will worship a god, or they will worship *the* God! Their souls are depending on whether or not we choose to remember and teach them these things!

Deuteronomy 5:28 *And the LORD heard the voice of your words, when ye spake unto me; and the LORD said unto me, I have heard the voice of the words of this people, which they have spoken unto thee: they have well said all that they have spoken.* **29** *O that there were such an heart in them, that they would fear me, and keep all my commandments always, that it might be well with them, and with their children for ever!*

"O THAT THERE WERE SUCH AN HEART IN THEM"

God heard the words of the people, and God saw the hearts of the people. The children of Israel said all the right things, but what was being said was contrary to what was in their hearts. There are many Christians who say things to sound spiritual but don't back it up with actions. For out of the heart comes the issues of life!

Deuteronomy 7:9 *Know therefore that the LORD thy God, he is God, the faithful God, which keepeth covenant and mercy with them that love him and keep his commandments to a thousand generations;*

"HE IS GOD, THE FAITHFUL GOD"

Our God is not just any God; He is the faithful God! His promises are true. He has promised them that love Him and keep His commandments to be faithful to them even to a thousand generations!

Deuteronomy 8:2 *And thou shalt remember all the way which the LORD thy God led thee these forty years in the wilderness, to humble thee, and to prove thee, to know what was in thine heart, whether thou wouldest keep his commandments, or no.*

"TO HUMBLE THEE, AND TO PROVE THEE, TO KNOW WHAT WAS IN THINE HEART, WHETHER THOU WOULDEST KEEP HIS COMMANDMENTS, OR NO"

Sometimes life is just life, and sometimes God intentionally puts us through trials to see how we react! Sometimes we need to be humbled before God before He can use us. Sometimes it is to prove ourselves in that we are able to withstand. Sometimes it has to soften a hardened heart, and sometimes it is just simply to see if we are truly tuned into His commands! How quickly we are distracted in the midst of a trial! Let us stay focused on the Lord even in the wilderness of our daily lives!

Deuteronomy 11:27 *A blessing, if ye obey the commandments of the LORD your God, which I command you this day:*

"A BLESSING, IF YE OBEY THE COMMANDMENTS OF THE LORD YOUR GOD"

Give and it shall be given unto you! A concept that is carried out throughout scripture. In this case it requires so little, and yet the reward is so much more than we deserve. The concept is simply this: if we will but simply obey, God will bless, and yet, how often do we fail and miss out on what God wanted to give us?

Deuteronomy 12:28 *Observe and hear all these words which I command thee, that it may go well with thee, and with thy children after thee for ever, when thou doest that which is good and right in the sight of the LORD thy God.*

"OBSERVE AND HEAR ALL THESE WORDS WHICH I COMMAND THEE"

Doing that which is right in God's eyes is not just for the here and now but for the generations to come. We are called to raise up a Godly generation. If we will not follow God's commands for our sake, then let us do it for our children's sake.

Deuteronomy 13:17 *And there shall cleave nought of the cursed thing to thine hand: that the LORD may turn from the fierceness of his anger, and shew thee mercy, and have compassion upon thee, and multiply thee, as he hath sworn unto thy fathers;*

"AND THERE SHALL CLEAVE NOUGHT OF THE CURSED THING TO THINE HAND"

The warning has been given. Covetousness can lead to destruction. For what does it profit a man if he gain the whole world and yet lose his own soul? The future destruction of Jericho will bring to light such a story in that of Achan. All was to be destroyed by fire, but Achan's greed brought sin into the camp!

Deuteronomy 14:23 *And thou shalt eat before the LORD thy God, in the place which he shall choose to place his name there, the tithe of thy corn, of thy wine, and of thine oil, and the firstlings of thy herds and of thy flocks; that thou mayest learn to fear the LORD thy God always.*

"IN THE PLACE WHICH HE SHALL CHOOSE TO PLACE HIS NAME THERE"

Where God chooses to put His name there, we ought to be content. They were not to move until the cloud by day or fire by night moved. We are called to serve. We follow the Master. Where He leads, I will follow!

Deuteronomy 16:17 *Every man shall give as he is able, according to the blessing of the LORD thy God which he hath given thee.*

"EVERY MAN SHALL GIVE AS HE IS ABLE"

God does not ask anything of us above and beyond that which we are able. We are asked only to give that which we are able to give. More specifically, we are only able to give as God has given to us. It is the man whom God has blessed whose selfishness and greed become idolatry and a stumbling block between himself and the Lord!

Deuteronomy 20:4 *For the LORD your God is he that goeth with you, to fight for you against your enemies, to save you.*

"FOR THE LORD YOUR GOD IS HE THAT GOETH WITH YOU"

What a great reminder that when we face opposition in our lives, the LORD GOD is with us to fight for us. When it seems like an impossible task, nothing is impossible with God! If God be for us, then who can be against us?

Deuteronomy 23:14 *For the LORD thy God walketh in the midst of thy camp, to deliver thee, and to give up thine enemies before thee; therefore shall thy camp be holy: that he see no unclean thing in thee, and turn away from thee.*

"FOR THE LORD THY GOD WALKETH IN THE MIDST OF THY CAMP"

A declaration to keep your dwelling place holy. The enemy is watching even in defeat. That we do not give ammunition to the enemy for later use, let us not be a stumbling block to anyone on the outside looking in!

Deuteronomy 26:11 *And thou shalt rejoice in every good thing which the LORD thy God hath given unto thee, and unto thine house, thou, and the Levite, and the stranger that is among you.*

"AND THOU SHALT REJOICE IN EVERY GOOD THING WHICH THE LORD THY GOD HATH GIVEN UNTO THE THEE"

The Christian has much to be thankful for; if not in this life, then surely we are to be thankful for that which is to come! Let us take a moment to simply look around us at all the Lord has given us and be thankful!

———————————————————

Deuteronomy 27:16 *Cursed be he that setteth light by his father or his mother. And all the people shall say, Amen.*

"CURSED BE HE THAT SETTETH LIGHT BY HIS FATHER OR HIS MOTHER"

Cursed be the child who feels the desire to correct, disrespect, rebuke, or dishonor a parent, especially in a public forum. The fifth commandment clearly states that children are to give honor to their parents!

———————————————————

Deuteronomy 28:2 *And all these blessings shall come on thee, and overtake thee, if thou shalt hearken unto the voice of the LORD thy God.*

"AND ALL THESE BLESSINGS SHALL COME ON THEE, AND OVERTAKE THEE"

A promise of either blessing or cursing. Those that diligently seek Him are overtaken with blessings. Those that refuse to follow God subject themselves to the harshest and most vile diseases and plagues. Which would you have, an overwhelming amount of blessings or the botch of Egypt?

———————————————————

Deuteronomy 29:9 *Keep therefore the words of this covenant, and do them, that ye may prosper in all that ye do.*

"THAT YE MAY PROSPER IN ALL THAT YE DO"

Do right! Always and in time, God will pour out His blessings. If we will but simply adhere to His Word and apply it to our everyday life, God's promise is that we will prosper in all that we do!

Deuteronomy 29:29 *The secret things belong unto the LORD our God: but those things which are revealed belong unto us and to our children for ever, that we may do all the words of this law.*

"THE SECRET THINGS BELONG UNTO THE LORD OUR GOD"

The future is for God to know and Him only. Though we cannot see what tomorrow holds, we certainly know Who holds tomorrow. Future events are revealed to us in His time. We are simply instructed to follow His Word.

Deuteronomy 30:15 *See, I have set before thee this day life and good, and death and evil;*

"LIFE AND GOOD, AND DEATH AND EVIL"

This day has been set before you. You must choose to either do good or to do evil. With every circumstance we encounter in life, a choice must be made: those choices could be a matter of life and death, whether it be physical or spiritual!

Deuteronomy 30:19 *I call heaven and earth to record this day against you, that I have set before you life and death, blessing and cursing: therefore choose life, that both thou and thy seed may live:*

"THEREFORE CHOOSE LIFE"

God has set before us life and death, both in the physical and spiritual form! We have the ability to choose the path that we travel. Let us choose life!

Deuteronomy 32:1 *Give ear, O ye heavens, and I will speak; and hear, O earth, the words of my mouth. 2 My doctrine shall drop as the rain, my speech shall distil as the dew, as the small rain upon the tender herb, and as the showers upon the grass: 3 Because I will publish the name of the LORD: ascribe ye greatness unto our God. 4 He is the Rock, his work is perfect: for all his ways are judgment: a God of truth and without iniquity, just and right is he.*

"MY DOCTRINE SHALL DROP AS THE RAIN"

OH PREACHER! THAT OUR DOCTRINE WOULD DROP LIKE RAIN!

Deuteronomy 32:31 *For their rock is not as our Rock, even our enemies themselves being judges.*

"FOR THEIR ROCK IS NOT AS OUR ROCK"

That which they stand on spiritually, those things in which they trust and have faith in, they are manmade and will surely fail! For who can stand against the King of kings and Lord of lords?

Deuteronomy 32:47 *For it is not a vain thing for you; because it is your life: and through this thing ye shall prolong your days in the land, whither ye go over Jordan to possess it.*

"FOR IT IS NOT A VAIN THING FOR YOU; BECAUSE IT IS YOUR LIFE"

Moses instructs the people to adhere to the law given by God Himself. God's laws are not in vain; but rather, to adhere to them is life itself. Christ himself stated, "It is written, Man shall not live by bread alone, but by every word that proceedeth out of the mouth of God." To have life more abundantly, it is imperative that we adhere to God's Word.

Deuteronomy 33:26 *There is none like unto the God of Jeshurun, who rideth upon the heaven in thy help, and in his excellency on the sky.*

"THERE IS NONE LIKE UNTO THE GOD OF JESHURAN"

JESHURAN a poetic term for Israel, meaning "to exalt, to lift up, or elevate." The time had come, and now the children of Israel would begin to take the place in a land flowing with milk and honey. The God who rides on the winds of Heaven will be their help and their guide.

GLEANINGS FROM THE BOOK OF JOSHUA

Joshua 3:3 *And they commanded the people, saying, When ye see the ark of the covenant of the LORD your God, and the priests the Levites bearing it, then ye shall remove from your place, and go after it.*

"THEN YE SHALL REMOVE FROM YOUR PLACE, AND GO AFTER IT"

When ye see the ark of God being carried throughout the camp, you are to rise up and follow it. Too often we jump the gun, so to speak, and move before God is ready for us to move. We must be patient and wait for God to move. We are called to follow Him, and to do so, we must wait on the Lord!

Joshua 4:24 *That all the people of the earth might know the hand of the LORD, that it is mighty: that ye might fear the LORD your God for ever.*

"THAT YE MIGHT FEAR THE LORD YOUR GOD FOR EVER"

The problem with society today is a lack of fear for God almighty! The fear of the Lord and faith go hand in hand. We must trust in His mighty hand to lead and guide us on our way and yet fear the consequences if we do not!

Joshua 7:25 *And Joshua said, Why hast thou troubled us? the LORD shall trouble thee this day. And all Israel stoned him with stones, and burned them with fire, after they had stoned them with stones.*

"AND JOSHUA SAID, WHY HAST THOU TROUBLED US"

This is in regard to the sin of Achan, who hid a garment, two hundred shekels of silver, and a wedge of gold worth fifty shekels in weight. His actions troubled not only his immediate household but all of Israel. A reminder to us all that our actions have a ripple effect that reaches further than what we might expect!

Joshua 9:14 *And the men took of their victuals, and asked not counsel at the mouth of the LORD.*

"AND ASKED NOT COUNSEL AT THE MOUTH OF THE LORD"

The Gibeonites tricked Joshua into a treaty to avoid being destroyed by the children of Israel. Joshua's mistake was not seeking counsel, especially that of the Lord. There is great wisdom in the counsel of Godly people and even more so ought we to seek God's will in our everyday doings.

Joshua 11:15 *As the LORD commanded Moses his servant, so did Moses command Joshua, and so did Joshua; he left nothing undone of all that the LORD commanded Moses.*

"SO DID JOSHUA; HE LEFT NOTHING UNDONE OF ALL THAT THE LORD COMMANDED MOSES"

Joshua left nothing undone! It is truly a great attribute and testimony of a child of God to finish what they start. An unfinished task may reveal one's true character

---

Joshua 14:12 *Now therefore give me this mountain, whereof the LORD spake in that day; for thou heardest in that day how the Anakims were there, and that the cities were great and fenced: if so be the LORD will be with me, then I shall be able to drive them out, as the LORD said.*

"THEN I SHALL BE ABLE TO DRIVE THEM OUT, AS THE LORD SAID"

Let us finish what we start! Let us leave nothing undone! No matter how large the task or how hard the climb might be, let us say, "GIVE ME THIS MOUNTAIN!" Let us get it done today!

Joshua 19:50 *According to the word of the LORD they gave him the city which he asked, even Timnathserah in mount Ephraim: and he built the city, and dwelt therein.*

"ACCORDING TO THE WORD OF THE LORD THEY GAVE HIM THE CITY WHICH HE ASKED"

It was Joshua and Caleb who gave a good report to Moses after spying out the land. Only these two would exhibit true strength and courage. Much is made about Caleb and his cry, "I WANT THAT MOUNTAIN," but Joshua too had a choice of land as was promised by God. He simply chose a city up on a hillside amongst his people, the tribe of Ephraim. He was a warrior full of strength and courage, but perhaps one of Joshua's greatest attributes is too often overlooked: humility!

Joshua 20:9 *These were the cities appointed for all the children of Israel, and for the stranger that sojourneth among them, that whosoever killeth any person at unawares might flee thither, and not die by the hand of the avenger of blood, until he stood before the congregation.*

"UNTIL HE STOOD BEFORE THE CONGREGATION"

Justice is a key component in who God is. Therefore, someone who was accused of a crime was given the right to live safely until his case could be heard. We should always act accordingly and in a just manner: for this, too, is a character trait of a Christian.

Joshua 22:5 *But take diligent heed to do the commandment and the law, which Moses the servant of the LORD charged you, to love the LORD your God, and to walk in all his ways, and to keep his commandments, and to cleave unto him, and to serve him with all your heart and with all your soul.*

"BUT TAKE DILIGENT HEED TO DO THE COMMANDMENT AND THE LAW"

A charge from Joshua to be diligent in serving the Lord! A great recipe for service this is! To love the Lord, to walk with the Lord, to keep the Lord's commandments, to cleave to the Lord, and to serve the Lord with all our hearts!

Joshua 23:3 *And ye have seen all that the LORD your God hath done unto all these nations because of you; for the LORD your God is he that hath fought for you.*

'FOR THE LORD YOUR GOD IS HE THAT HATH FOUGHT FOR YOU"

Joshua's final words to the children of Israel. Joshua challenges the people to not forget what God has done nor forget His law. Sadly, America has forgotten her roots. Israel's forsaking of God's Word led to their captivity and future problems. Let us pray that America will seek God's face and not forget how God has blessed her as a nation.

GLEANINGS FROM THE BOOK OF JUDGES

Judges 2:2 *And ye shall make no league with the inhabitants of this land; ye shall throw down their altars: but ye have not obeyed my voice: why have ye done this?*

"WHY HAVE YE DONE THIS"

Why have you made treaties with unbelievers? Why have you taken their false doctrine as your own? Why have you disobeyed my voice? These are reasonable questions to God's people. The day God approaches His people and asks, "Why have ye done this?" do you have an answer?

Judges 3:21 *And Ehud put forth his left hand, and took the dagger from his right thigh, and thrust it into his belly:* **22** *And the haft also went in after the blade; and the fat closed upon the blade, so that he could not draw the dagger out of his belly; and the dirt came out.*

"AND THE DIRT CAME OUT"

The Word of God is compared to a two-edged sword! When the Word of God goes in, the dirt comes out!

Judges 5:2 *Praise ye the LORD for the avenging of Israel, when the people willingly offered themselves.*

"WHEN THE PEOPLE WILLINGLY OFFERED THEMSELVES"

God can and will do amazing things with people who willingly allow Him to do so. Shamgar had but a simple ox goad. David had but a sling. Deborah had words of encouragement. No matter how great or small of talent someone may or may not have, it is the willing heart that God uses.

Judges 5:8 *They chose new gods; then was war in the gates: was there a shield or spear seen among forty thousand in Israel?*

"THEN WAS WAR IN THE GATES"

Trouble came only after they chose new gods. They once served the one true GOD but made a choice to serve other gods. Could it be that the trouble we have in our lives is brought in by who we worship? For we bring trouble upon ourselves when we forsake the one true GOD.

Judges 5:16 *Why abodest thou among the sheepfolds, to hear the bleatings of the flocks? For the divisions of Reuben there were great searchings of heart.*

"WHY ABODEST THOU AMONG THE SHEEPFOLDS"

The tribe of Reuben is rebuked by Deborah in this passage for caring more about their herds than fighting for their nation! Let that sink in! Let's get in the fight! Is there something more important than a lost soul?

Judges 10:14 *Go and cry unto the gods which ye have chosen; let them deliver you in the time of your tribulation.*

"LET THEM DELIVER YOU IN THE TIME OF YOUR TRIBULATION"

It has often been said that there are no atheists in a foxhole! God rebukes the children of Israel for crying out to God only in their distress. Certainly, God hears our cries when we need Him most, but He wants to hear from us when times are good. Too often, we use God as simply our way out rather than our WAY!

Judges 10:16 *And they put away the strange gods from among them, and served the LORD: and his soul was grieved for the misery of Israel.*

"AND THEY PUT AWAY THE STRANGE GODS FROM AMONG THEM, AND SERVED THE LORD"

Could it be that we have strange gods that we serve and love even more than our Lord? That addiction or habit that keeps us from serving the Lord with all our heart, soul and mind! God's desire for us is that we put away those things and serve Him only.

Judges 13:12 *And Manoah said, Now let thy words come to pass. How shall we order the child, and how shall we do unto him?*

"HOW SHALL WE ORDER THE CHILD, AND HOW SHALL WE DO UNTO HIM?"

Manoah questioned the angel of the Lord in regard to how they should raise their child Samson. Likewise, parents today ought to seek God's face in regard to the raising of their children. Train them up in the way they should go; for when they are old, they will not depart from it!

Judges 16:20 *And she said, The Philistines be upon thee, Samson. And he awoke out of his sleep, and said, I will go out as at other times before, and shake myself. And he wist not that the LORD was departed from him.*

"AND HE WIST NOT THAT THE LORD WAS DEPARTED FROM HIM"

Many a man of God has stepped behind the pulpit ready to do spiritual battle, all the while unaware that the Lord has departed from him. Too often we become dependent on our own strength instead of relying on the Lord.

Judges 17:6 *In those days there was no king in Israel, but every man did that which was right in his own eyes.*

"BUT EVERY MAN DID THAT WHICH WAS RIGHT IN HIS OWN EYES"

A phrase that is stated many times throughout the book of Judges. In this case, in reference to personal idolatry. A man named Micah invents his own religion and hires his own priest. How ironic; in the chapters that follow, the most gruesome acts in scripture are recorded. Personal religion has no basis in scripture but rather leads to an "anything goes" society.

Judges 17:9 *And Micah said unto him, Whence comest thou? And he said unto him, I am a Levite of Bethlehem- judah, and I go to sojourn where I may find a place. 10 And Micah said unto him, Dwell with me, and be unto me a father and a priest, and I will give thee ten shekels of silver by the year, and a suit of apparel, and thy victuals. So the Levite went in.*

"AND I GO TO SOJOURN WHERE I MAY FIND A PLACE"

The priest said, "I am a Levite...and I go to sojourn where I may find a place." He was then offered a good salary and comfortable surroundings serving for a man who also served false gods! Are you where you're supposed to be? Or are you just comfortable?

Judges 21:25 *In those days there was no king in Israel: every man did that which was right in his own eyes.*

"EVERY MAN DID THAT WHICH WAS RIGHT IN HIS OWN EYES"

How evident that is in today's society. Every man doing what they believe to be right! On the surface, it does not seem that wrong, but God's ways are not our ways. We should be diligently seeking God's direction in our lives, not living by impulse or feeling.

GLEANINGS FROM THE BOOK OF RUTH

Ruth 2:10 *Then she fell on her face, and bowed herself to the ground, and said unto him, Why have I found grace in thine eyes, that thou shouldest take knowledge of me, seeing I am a stranger?*

"THAT THOU SHOULDEST TAKE KNOWLEDGE OF ME,"

The story of the kinsman redeemer! Praise the Lord that He redeemed us! In Ruth 4:14, the women proclaimed to Naomi, "Blessed be the LORD, which hath not left thee this day without a kinsman." Praise the Lord that He did not leave us without a Redeemer! Lord, what have I done to deserve your grace and mercy? Thank God for the blood of Jesus that paid the price for our sin and redeemed us!

Ruth 4:14 *And the women said unto Naomi, Blessed be the LORD, which hath not left thee this day without a kinsman, that his name may be famous in Israel.*

"THAT HIS NAME MAY BE FAMOUS IN ISRAEL"

There are five women mentioned in the lineage of Jesus. Ruth is one of them. Naomi just a short time ago declared herself to be Mara, or bitter, and yet now she is full of joy once again. That her family name would be known in Israel is an understatement. For Ruth gave birth to Obed. Obed begat Jesse. Jesse begat David, who would be king!

GLEANINGS FROM THE BOOK OF 1 SAMUEL

1 Samuel 1:15 *And Hannah answered and said, No, my lord, I am a woman of a sorrowful spirit: I have drunk neither wine nor strong drink, but have poured out my soul before the LORD.*

"BUT HAVE POURED OUT MY SOUL BEFORE THE LORD"

Hannah was assumed drunk; for though her voice was not heard, her lips could be seen in conversation. When you are truly in the presence of God, you will pay no mind to what people think or say. Let us put aside the cares of this world but for just a moment, that we might pour out our soul's hurts and desires and lay them at His feet.

---

1 Samuel 2:3 *Talk no more so exceeding proudly; let not arrogancy come out of your mouth: for the LORD is a God of knowledge, and by him actions are weighed.*

"AND BY HIM ACTIONS ARE WEIGHED"

The phrase "actions speak louder than words" is proclaimed loud and clear in this verse. The proud and the arrogant are but just sounds coming from one's mouth, but God sees a man of action and takes notice!

---

1 Samuel 3:1 *And the child Samuel ministered unto the LORD before Eli. And the word of the LORD was precious in those days; there was no open vision.*

"AND THE WORD OF THE LORD WAS PRECIOUS IN THOSE DAYS"

This is to say that it was rare. Sad to say that even today, it seems that it is a rare thing to find a man of God who truly stands on God's Word. It is a rare thing to find a Christian who lives what they believe. When something is so rare, it becomes precious!

1 Samuel 6:7 *Now therefore make a new cart, and take two milch kine, on which there hath come no yoke, and tie the kine to the cart, and bring their calves home from them:*

"NOW THEREFORE MAKE A NEW CART"

In 2 Samuel 6, King David desires to transport the Ark of God back to Jerusalem. God had instructed that the Ark be carried on staves by the priesthood. David put the Ark on a new cart pulled by oxen. When the oxen stumbled, a man named Uzzah reached up to steady the cart, and God killed him. The new cart was a pagan practice instilled by the Philistines. Be careful that we do not replace what God has instructed with our own desires.

---

1 Samuel 8:7 *And the LORD said unto Samuel, Hearken unto the voice of the people in all that they say unto thee: for they have not rejected thee, but they have rejected me, that I should not reign over them.*

"BUT THEY HAVE REJECTED THEE"

People do not in general dislike Christian people; rather, they dislike the One that is in you. They dislike the One you serve and all He stands for. It is not us personally the world hates but the Christ whom we serve!

---

1 Samuel 9:27 *And as they were going down to the end of the city, Samuel said to Saul, Bid the servant pass on before us, (and he passed on,) but stand thou still a while, that I may shew thee the word of God.*

"BUT STAND THOU STILL A WHILE, THAT I MAY SHEW THEE THE WORD OF GOD"

Samuel told Saul to stand still for just a moment so that he might share the Word of God with him. It would do us well in the rush of our daily lives to just stand still for a moment and hear what God has to say to us!

---

1 Samuel 12:12 *And when ye saw that Nahash the king of the children of Ammon came against you, ye said unto me, Nay; but a king shall reign over us: when the LORD your God was your king.*

"WHEN THE LORD YOUR GOD WAS YOUR KING"

The words of Samuel at the coronation of king Saul. How bold Samuel was, for the people demanded a king when God was their king. Samuel declared that Saul was not the answer to their trouble but that they should turn their hearts toward God. As Christians, we must be careful not to allow leaders to dictate to us, as people, morals and values; for they may lead our community and nation, but God is our King!

---

1 Samuel 12:23 *Moreover as for me, God forbid that I should sin against the LORD in ceasing to pray for you: but I will teach you the good and the right way:*

"THAT I SHOULD SIN AGAINST THE LORD IN CEASING TO PRAY FOR YOU"

Men ought always to pray! Men ought always to pray without ceasing! How should we start the day? PRAY!

---

1 Samuel 16:7 *But the LORD said unto Samuel, Look not on his countenance, or on the height of his stature; because I have refused him: for the LORD seeth not as man seeth; for man looketh on the outward appearance, but the LORD looketh on the heart.*

"LOOK NOT ON HIS COUNTENANCE, OR ON THE HEIGHT OF HIS STATURE"

How quickly we judge a book by the cover! God loves the broken ones. He loves those that He can mold to His making. If God can turn a shepherd boy into a king, then what can He do with you and I? No matter the physical lacking someone may or may not have, God is the reader of hearts!

***

1 Samuel 17:10 *And the Philistine said, I defy the armies of Israel this day; give me a man, that we may fight together.*

"GIVE ME A MAN, THAT WE MAY FIGHT TOGETHER"

Goliath cries out, "Give me a man that we may fight!" Where are the men who are willing to fight for the cause of Christ? Where are the men who won't back down, even when it's not popular? Where are the men who will take a stand against those who defy the God of Israel?

***

1 Samuel 20:3 *And David sware moreover, and said, Thy father certainly knoweth that I have found grace in thine eyes; and he saith, Let not Jonathan know this, lest he be grieved: but truly as the LORD liveth, and as thy soul liveth, there is but a step between me and death.*

"THERE IS BUT A STEP BETWEEN ME AND DEATH"

Today could be your day to die! Are you ready? Have we done all that we can for the cause of Christ?

***

1 Samuel 23:9 *And David knew that Saul secretly practised mischief against him; and he said to Abiathar the priest, Bring hither the ephod.*

"AND DAVID KNEW THAT SAUL SECRETLY PRACTICED MISCHIEF AGAINST HIM"

David's response to Saul's plot to kill him. His response was not one of anger, revenge, or retaliation; rather, David turned to the Lord in prayer. It would do us as Christians well to follow the example of David and pray for those who seek to do us wrong.

---

1 Samuel 24:10 *Behold, this day thine eyes have seen how that the LORD had delivered thee today into mine hand in the cave: and some bade me kill thee: but mine eye spared thee; and I said, I will not put forth mine hand against my lord; for he is the LORD'S anointed.*

"FOR HE IS THE LORDS ANOINTED"

Even those called by God have come short of His glory. Though they fall short, that does not give others the right to come against them. If God called them, then God can remove them, in His time and in His way.

---

1 Samuel 25:28 *I pray thee, forgive the trespass of thine handmaid: for the LORD will certainly make my lord a sure house; because my lord fighteth the battles of the LORD, and evil hath not been found in thee all thy days.*

"FOR THE LORD WILL CERTAINLY MAKE MY LORD A SURE HOUSE; BECAUSE MY LORD FIGHTETH THE BATTLES OF THE LORD"

There is an old saying: "You might win the battle but lose the war." Sometimes in our daily life, we must pick and choose our battles. Not every battle we face is worth fighting, nor is the Lord glorified.

Such was the case for David and Nabal. David made the right choice to step back and let the Lord fight this particular battle!

---

1 Samuel 26:21 *Then said Saul, I have sinned: return, my son David: for I will no more do thee harm, because my soul was precious in thine eyes this day: behold, I have played the fool, and have erred exceedingly.*

"I HAVE PLAYED THE FOOL, AND HAVE ERRED EXCEEDINGLY"

Anger and jealousy can lead to foolish actions. A prime example is that of Saul. Jealous of David's accomplishments and popularity with the people, Saul sought to kill David. Saul's own admission: he had played the fool and had erred exceedingly.

---

1 Samuel 30:6 *And David was greatly distressed; for the people spake of stoning him, because the soul of all the people was grieved, every man for his sons and for his daughters: but David encouraged himself in the LORD his God.*

"BUT DAVID ENCOURAGED HIMSELF IN THE LORD"

David was under much stress and discouraged! When it seemed everyone was against him and life's trials seemed overwhelming, he found encouragement in the LORD! Let us likewise be encouraged today in the LORD OUR GOD!

GLEANINGS FROM THE BOOK OF 2 SAMUEL

2 Samuel 1:25 *How are the mighty fallen in the midst of the battle! O Jonathan, thou wast slain in thine high places.*

"HOW ARE THE MIGHTY FALLEN IN THE MIDST OF BATTLE"

David laments the loss of his dear friend Jonathan. He had died standing his ground with weapon in hand! Nothing greater can be said about a child of God when they die than that they died in the midst of battle serving the Lord!

---

2 Samuel 3:39 *And I am this day weak, though anointed king; and these men the sons of Zeruiah be too hard for me: the LORD shall reward the doer of evil according to his wickedness.*

"THE LORD SHALL REWARD THE DOER OF EVIL ACCORDING TO HIS WICKEDNESS"

You will truly reap what you sow. The Lord will reward righteousness with blessing, and the doer of evil will likewise be rewarded for his wickedness. Blessing? No, but rather chastisement.

---

2 Samuel 7:2 *That the king said unto Nathan the prophet, See now, I dwell in an house of cedar, but the ark of God dwelleth within curtains.*

"I DWELL IN AN HOUSE OF CEDAR, BUT THE ARK OF GOD DWELLETH WITHIN CURTAINS"

David sees that his personal home is more comfortable and lavish than the curtains behind which the Ark of God dwells. David's desire is to honor and give God a dwelling place that is better than that in which he himself lives. Oh, that the child of God would have such a heart in all things in that we also had a desire to honor God with all that we have and do.

2 Samuel 7:22 *Wherefore thou art great, O LORD God: for there is none like thee, neither is there any God beside thee, according to all that we have heard with our ears.*

"WHEREFORE THOU ART GREAT"

Reflecting on the shape of this world and all of its violence and dysfunction, I cannot help but pause for just a moment and say HOW GREAT IS OUR GOD; though it seems at times that the world is spinning off its axis, our God is still in control!

2 Samuel 11:1 *And it came to pass, after the year was expired, at the time when kings go forth to battle, that David sent Joab, and his servants with him, and all Israel; and they destroyed the children of Ammon, and besieged Rabbah. But David tarried still at Jerusalem.*

"AND IT CAME TO PASS, AFTER THE YEAR WAS EXPIRED, AT THE TIME WHEN KINGS GO FORTH TO BATTLE"

In those days, battles were planned. The time and place were pre-arranged. David, being king, should have been on the battlefield; but rather, we see him at his house relaxing. David failed to address his responsibility, and his idleness led to his fall into sin. Let us not be idle today; but rather, let us be busy about the Father's business!

2 Samuel 13:13 *And I, whither shall I cause my shame to go? and as for thee, thou shalt be as one of the fools in Israel. Now therefore, I pray thee, speak unto the king; for he will not withhold me from thee.*

"THOU SHALT BE AS ONE OF THE FOOLS IN ISRAEL"

Amnon's incestuous relationship with his half-sister Tamar recorded. Tamar's response is to be noted here. The most vile acts of immorality are but viewed as foolishness to those looking on. Is it any wonder that the United States is losing respect from other nations, and we are viewed as fools?

---

2 Samuel 14:32 *And Absalom answered Joab, Behold, I sent unto thee, saying, Come hither, that I may send thee to the king, to say, Wherefore am I come from Geshur? it had been good for me to have been there still: now therefore let me see the king's face; and if there be any iniquity in me, let him kill me.*

"NOW THEREFORE LET ME SEE THE KING'S FACE"

David's forgiveness only went so far. Absalom was allowed to return home but was not allowed to stand before the king. Though Absalom was in the wrong, he desired to see the king's face. What a great truth. When we likewise find ourselves in the wrong, let us desire to see the king's face!

---

2 Samuel 16:12 *It may be that the LORD will look on mine affliction, and that the LORD will requite me good for his cursing this day.*

"THAT THE LORD WILL REQUITE ME GOOD FOR HIS CURSING THIS DAY"

How do we act when people curse us? It could be that we need do nothing; but rather, it is for our better good to just give it to the Lord!

---

2 Samuel 18:33 *And the king was much moved, and went up to the chamber over the gate, and wept: and as he went, thus he said, O my son Absalom, my son, my son Absalom! would God I had died for thee, O Absalom, my son, my son!*

"O MY SON ABSALOM, MY SON, MY SON ABSALOM! WOULD GOD I HAD DIED FOR THEE"

Even after all that Absalom had done to his father, David loved and wept for his son! Many a child has broken the heart of a parent and yet is blind to the love and sacrifice the parent has for the child. Likewise, how do we take for granted Christ's love for us and all that God does for His children!

---

2 Samuel 19:28 *For all of my father's house were but dead men before my lord the king: yet didst thou set thy servant among them that did eat at thine own table. What right therefore have I yet to cry any more unto the king?*

"WHAT RIGHT HAVE I YET TO CRY ANYMORE UNTO THE KING"

Mephibosheth greets David upon return after the death of Absalom. The kingdom is in shambles, and the agreement between Mephibosheth and David was not held up by Absalom. Yet there is no complaint on behalf of Mephibosheth. What right do we have to complain? For God has in times past poured out His blessings and will do so again!

---

2 Samuel 22:4 *I will call on the LORD, who is worthy to be praised: so shall I be saved from mine enemies.*

"I WILL CALL ON THE LORD, WHO IS WORTHY TO BE PRAISED"

I wonder whom others call on in their time of need. I call on the Lord! The King of Kings and Lord of Lords! For He alone is worthy to be praised, and by Him and Him alone may I claim victory over my enemies!

---

2 Samuel 23:10 *He arose, and smote the Philistines until his hand was weary, and his hand clave unto the sword: and the LORD wrought a great victory that day; and the people returned after him only to spoil.*

"AND HIS HAND CLAVE UNTO THE SWORD"

Eleazar was called a mighty man by King David; for when he was in battle, he fought so hard and so long that his hand clave to the sword. In other words, his hand became one with the sword! Oh, that we treated that two-edged sword called the Word of God in such manner; that we would cleave to it so closely that when the world looks at us, Christ is revealed!

GLEANINGS FROM THE BOOK OF 1 KINGS

1 Kings 2:3 *And keep the charge of the LORD thy God, to walk in his ways, to keep his statutes, and his commandments, and his judgments, and his testimonies, as it is written in the law of Moses, that thou mayest prosper in all that thou doest, and whithersoever thou turnest thyself:*

"THAT THOU MAYEST PROSPER IN ALL THAT THOU DOEST"

David challenges Solomon to adhere to walk in God's way and to keep God's statutes, commandments, judgments, and testimonies. The child of God who does these things is given a promise of prosperity. Prosperity is not necessarily wealth and riches but the fullness of God's blessings poured out.

---

1 Kings 3:12 *Behold, I have done according to thy words: lo, I have given thee a wise and an understanding heart; so that there was none like thee before thee, neither after thee shall any arise like unto thee.*

"I HAVE GIVEN THEE A WISE AND AN UNDERSTANDING HEART"

Solomon's request was not just for wisdom but for an understanding heart. Without love, all the wealth and understanding are nothing. The very fact that Solomon requested the heart with wisdom was wise in and of itself! Let us also seek wisdom and understanding, but may we have a Godly heart to support all that we may endeavor!

---

1 Kings 3:28 *And all Israel heard of the judgment which the king had judged; and they feared the king: for they saw that the wisdom of God was in him, to do judgment.*

"FOR THEY SAW THAT THE WISDOM OF GOD WAS IN HIM, TO DO JUDGEMENT"

All who encountered Solomon saw the wisdom of God in him! Oh, that every Christian would strive to have that kind of Godly wisdom. Not wisdom that is judgmental or divisive but rather that is respected and glorifying of our Lord!

---

1 Kings 8:12 *Then spake Solomon, The LORD said that he would dwell in the thick darkness.*

"THE LORD SAID THAT HE WOULD DWELL IN THE THICK DARKNESS"

Upon reading this verse, I am reminded that even in the darkness, there we may find His presence! No matter the trial that you are facing, know that the God on the mountain is also the God of the valley, and the God of the day is also the God of the night. For the Lord said that He would dwell in the thick darkness!

---

1 Kings 8:27 *But will God indeed dwell on the earth? behold, the heaven and heaven of heavens cannot contain thee; how much less this house that I have builded?*

"BEHOLD THE HEAVEN AND HEAVEN OF HEAVENS CANNOT CONTAIN THEE"

Solomon, during his dedication speech acknowledged that as grand and glorious as the temple was, it was still not adequate to contain His glory! May we likewise remember that we are bought tools in the Master's hand, and He is bigger and greater than anything we have to offer!

1 Kings 15:14 *But the high places were not removed: nevertheless Asa's heart was perfect with the LORD all his days.*

"BUT THE HIGH PLACES WERE NOT REMOVED"

For there is none righteous, no not one. As Godly as one might think themselves to be, none of us are without fault! Let us examine ourselves and confess our sin that we may strive to have a perfect heart before our Lord!

---

1 Kings 18:15 *And Elijah said, As the LORD of hosts liveth, before whom I stand, I will surely shew myself unto him to day.*

"BEFORE WHOM I STAND"

Elijah declared that he stood for the Lord! Just where do you stand today?

---

1 Kings 18:17 *And it came to pass, when Ahab saw Elijah, that Ahab said unto him, Art thou he that troubleth Israel?*

"ART THOU HE THAT TROUBLETH ISRAEL"

Ahab, an ungodly king, declares that Elijah, the prophet of God, is troubling Israel. How is it that morality and good behavior is troublesome to a nation? When did pagan worship, drunkenness, and sin become the norm? Right is still right, and wrong is still wrong. Perhaps it's time the Christians stir up some trouble.

---

1 Kings 18:21 *And Elijah came unto all the people, and said, How long halt ye between two opinions? if the LORD be God, follow him: but if Baal, then follow him. And the people answered him not a word.*

"HOW LONG HALT YE BETWEEN TWO OPINIONS"

Many a man will try to walk on top of a picket fence; and yet sooner or later, he will fall off to one side or the other! Man cannot serve two masters; he will either give his loyalty to the one or the other! How long will we say we serve the Lord and yet live for the devil?

---

1 Kings 21:25 *But there was none like unto Ahab, which did sell himself to work wickedness in the sight of the LORD, whom Jezebel his wife stirred up.*

"WHICH DID SELL HIMSELF TO WORK WICKEDNESS"

Ahab sold himself in his wickedness! Sin has a price! How much have you paid? What will you pay today? Just how much will it cost you? Eventually, Ahab would pay with his life! God has called us to righteousness, not wickedness!

---

1 Kings 22:8 *And the king of Israel said unto Jehoshaphat, There is yet one man, Micaiah the son of Imlah, by whom we may enquire of the LORD: but I hate him; for he doth not prophesy good concerning me, but evil. And Jehoshaphat said, Let not the king say so.*

"BUT I HATE HIM"

Jehoshaphat and Ahab had a common enemy in that of Syria. Jehoshaphat recommended that they seek counsel before going to war. Ahab called on four hundred prophets, who all gave the same counsel. Jehoshaphat requested that they enquire of a prophet of the Lord. Ahab says there is one, "but I hate him." The world hates truth. Though the whole world agrees, Lord, give me strength to stand on the truth.

GLEANINGS FROM THE BOOK OF 2 KINGS

2 Kings 1:16 *And he said unto him, Thus saith the LORD, Forasmuch as thou hast sent messengers to enquire of Baalzebub the god of Ekron, is it not because there is no God in Israel to enquire of his word? therefore thou shalt not come down off that bed on which thou art gone up, but shalt surely die.*

"IS IT NOT BECAUSE THERE IS NO GOD IN ISRAEL TO ENQUIRE OF HIS WORD"

The reason some choose to take certain action that seems appalling to those of us that are Christians is not because there is not a God in Heaven to enquire of. Perhaps the bad decisions made by some is because a Christian has failed to tell them of the God in Heaven.

———————————————

2 Kings 4:26 *Run now, I pray thee, to meet her, and say unto her, Is it well with thee? is it well with thy husband? is it well with the child? And she answered, It is well.*

"AND SHE ANSWERED, IT IS WELL"

How interesting this passage of scripture is; for when asked how she was doing, this Shunammite woman replied, "It is well." Her son was dead, and yet even in a time of distress and loss, she replied, "It is well." Can we likewise say it is well, or will we cave under the stress of this daily life?

———————————————

2 Kings 6:17 *And Elisha prayed, and said, LORD, I pray thee, open his eyes, that he may see. And the LORD opened the eyes of the young man; and he saw: and, behold, the mountain was full of horses and chariots of fire round about Elisha.*

"I PRAY THEE, OPEN HIS EYES, THAT HE MAY SEE"

Elisha's prayer for his servant to God is that he might see that which is spiritual! Oh, that we might fall to our knees and pray for the spiritual awakening of our nation, our families, our neighbors, and our friends!

---

2 Kings 7:9 *Then they said one to another, We do not well: this day is a day of good tidings, and we hold our peace: if we tarry till the morning light, some mischief will come upon us: now therefore come, that we may go and tell the king's household.*

"THIS DAY IS A DAY OF GOOD TIDINGS AND WE HOLD OUR PEACE"

Four lepers, who had nothing to live for, knew that they could not remain silent, for they had good news! We who have our health and well-being also have good news, yet we keep it to ourselves! This day is a day of good tidings, so let's share the good news with someone today!

---

2 Kings 10:10 *Know now that there shall fall unto the earth nothing of the word of the LORD, which the LORD spake concerning the house of Ahab: for the LORD hath done that which he spake by his servant Elijah.*

"KNOW NOW THAT THERE SHALL FALL UNTO THE EARTH NOTHING OF THE WORD OF THE LORD"

In other words, when God speaks, His words are not wasted falling to the earth just to be trampled upon. When God speaks, you can be assured His words will take effect!

---

2 Kings 11:17 *And Jehoiada made a covenant between the LORD and the king and the people, that they should be the LORD'S people; between the king also and the people.*

"AND JEHOIADA MADE A COVENANT BETWEEN THE LORD AND THE KING AND THE PEOPLE"

Jehoiada made a commitment to serve the Lord, a renewed commitment to walk and to serve the one and only true God of Israel. Perhaps it's time for America to renew its commitment to the Lord!

------

2 Kings 14:6 *But the children of the murderers he slew not: according unto that which is written in the book of the law of Moses, wherein the LORD commanded, saying, The fathers shall not be put to death for the children, nor the children be put to death for the fathers; but every man shall be put to death for his own sin.*

"BUT EVERY MAN SHALL BE PUT TO DEATH FOR HIS OWN SIN"

God does not send anyone to Hell; but rather, it is a choice made by man. God has provided a sacrifice to take our place. He has redeemed us unto His own. The unpardonable sin is to reject Christ. If one dies in his sin and spends an eternity in hell, then that is his own doing.

------

2 Kings 17:9 *And the children of Israel did secretly those things that were not right against the LORD their God, and they built them high places in all their cities, from the tower of the watchmen to the fenced city.*

"AND THE CHILDREN OF ISRAEL DID SECRETLY THOSE THINGS THAT WERE NOT RIGHT AGAINST THE LORD THEIR GOD"

Or so they thought! What they tried to hide in secret, God saw and allowed Syria to take them captive! Just because we do something in secret does not mean it will not have consequences!

------

2 Kings 18:6 *For he clave to the LORD, and departed not from following him, but kept his commandments, which the LORD commanded Moses.*

"HE CLAVE TO THE LORD AND DEPARTED NOT FROM FOLLOWING HIM"

Who or what are you clinging to? Whom do you follow?

---

2 Kings 19:27 *But I know thy abode, and thy going out, and thy coming in, and thy rage against me.*

"BUT I KNOW"

God said, "I know your abode, your current circumstance." He knows all of our doings on a daily basis! He knows when we defy Him! He knows all that we do on a daily basis. Do we walk in confidence knowing that He knows all, or do we walk in shame knowing He knows our daily actions?

---

2 Kings 20:1 *In those days was Hezekiah sick unto death. And the prophet Isaiah the son of Amoz came to him, and said unto him, Thus saith the LORD, Set thine house in order; for thou shalt die, and not live.*

"THUS SAITH THE LORD, SET THINE HOUSE IN ORDER"

Do all things decently and in order. This includes death. Many a man has left behind confusion and trial for their remaining loved ones to deal with. It is a good thing to have your house in order before leaving this earth.

---

2 Kings 21:14 *And I will forsake the remnant of mine inheritance, and deliver them into the hand of their enemies; and they shall become a prey and a spoil to all their enemies;*

"AND THEY SHALL BECOME A PREY AND A SPOIL TO ALL THEIR ENEMIES"

Manasseh was such an evil king that God said that the nation of Israel had become more evil than even their pagan enemies. Josiah would later tear down all the altars of pagan worship and renew the covenant as it was written with God. However, there are consequences to a nation's actions and morals. If America does not renew her covenant, she too will fall.

---

2 Kings 23:2 *And the king went up into the house of the LORD, and all the men of Judah and all the inhabitants of Jerusalem with him, and the priests, and the prophets, and all the people, both small and great: and he read in their ears all the words of the book of the covenant which was found in the house of the LORD.*

"AND HE READ IN THEIR EARS ALL THE WORDS OF THE BOOK OF THE COVENANT WHICH WAS FOUND IN THE HOUSE OF THE LORD"

King Josiah, after reading what Gods Word said, then applied and put into action God's Word. Something that stands out to me is the word ALL! He read ALL of it! He shared ALL of it with the people, and he took ALL of it to heart! We must likewise take ALL of the Word of God and apply it to our hearts and everyday life!

GLEANINGS FROM THE BOOK OF 1 CHRONICLES

1 Chronicles 4:10 *And Jabez called on the God of Israel, saying, Oh that thou wouldest bless me indeed, and enlarge my coast, and that thine hand might be with me, and that thou wouldest keep me from evil, that it may not grieve me! And God granted him that which he requested.*

"AND GOD GRANTED HIM THAT WHICH HE REQUESTED"

Verse nine of this same chapter says that Jabez was more honorable than his brethren! Let us live honorably before God if we expect Him to grant our request!

---

1 Chronicles 5:19 *And they made war with the Hagarites, with Jetur, and Nephish, and Nodab. 20 And they were helped against them, and the Hagarites were delivered into their hand, and all that were with them: for they cried to God in the battle, and he was intreated of them; because they put their trust in him.*

"THEY CRIED TO GOD IN THE BATTLE"

Is it not great to know that in the heat of the battle, we can cry out to our GOD? Whatever the trial you may be facing today, let us take the time to call on our GOD!

---

1 Chronicles 5:22 *For there fell down many slain, because the war was of God. And they dwelt in their steads until the captivity.*

"BECAUSE THE WAR WAS OF GOD"

As I read this verse, I couldn't help but be reminded of the old saying, "Pick your battles, for you may win the battle but lose the war." Take great care in choosing your battles, for if it is not of God, the casualties could be great!

1 Chronicles 11:18 *And the three brake through the host of the Philistines, and drew water out of the well of Bethlehem, that was by the gate, and took it, and brought it to David: but David would not drink of it, but poured it out to the Lord.*

"AND BROUGHT IT TO DAVID"

These three men snuck behind enemy lines just to bring King David a drink of water from the well at Bethlehem. A selfless act, for sure, to go the extra mile for someone else. The actions of mighty men are often played out simply by putting others before themselves, no matter how great or small the deed.

1 Chronicles 14:15 *And it shall be, when thou shalt hear a sound of going in the tops of the mulberry trees, that then thou shalt go out to battle: for God is gone forth before thee to smite the host of the Philistines.*

"WHEN THOU SHALT HEAR A SOUND OF GOING"

When you hear the wind rustling in the tops of the trees, then march and go forth to battle. Though beautiful imagery, it does, however, bring to mind the moving of the Holy Spirit as a rushing wind. Too often we move in matters of our life without the Holy Spirit leading. Let us wait to hear the rustling in the tops of the trees before we move.

1 Chronicles 16:25 *For great is the LORD, and greatly to be praised: he also is to be feared above all gods.*

"FOR GREAT IS THE LORD, AND GREATLY TO BE PRAISED"

Many will acknowledge the greatness of our God but fail in the greatness of praise. Though all of our praise could not equal what is the greatness of our God, let us not remain silent, for He is worthy!

---

1 Chronicles 19:13 *Be of good courage, and let us behave ourselves valiantly for our people, and for the cities of our God: and let the LORD do that which is good in his sight.*

"AND LET US BEHAVE OURSELVES VALIANTLY FOR OUR PEOPLE"

As I read this, the thought came to my mind that Gods people should behave themselves in a courageous manner! We can face whatever comes our way with confidence, knowing that, whatever the outcome, God is in control!

---

1 Chronicles 22:16 *Of the gold, the silver, and the brass, and the iron, there is no number. Arise therefore, and be doing, and the LORD be with thee.*

"ARISE THEREFORE, AND BE DOING"

David instructed his son Solomon to finish what David had started. David had gathered together all the supplies needed to build the temple; however, it would be up to Solomon to build it. Every large task requires a first step. One must arise!

---

1 Chronicles 22:19 *Now set your heart and your soul to seek the LORD your God; arise therefore, and build ye the sanctuary of the LORD God, to bring the ark of the covenant of the LORD, and the holy vessels of God, into the house that is to be built to the name of the LORD.*

"NOW SET YOUR HEART AND YOUR SOUL TO SEEK THE LORD YOUR GOD"

Many a good deed has been done but minus the heart behind it! Serving God requires the heart and soul to be involved! Man looks on the outward appearance, but God sees the heart! For what or whom do you labor? For self? Or for the glory of God?

---

1 Chronicles 29:16 *O LORD our God, all this store that we have prepared to build thee an house for thine holy name cometh of thine hand, and is all thine own.*

"COMETH OF THINE HAND, AND IS ALL THINE OWN"

Many an individual has ignored the giving of offerings with the excuse of not having enough in their possession to give when, in reality, what they own is not theirs to begin with. To give away what is not ours to begin with suddenly becomes a very small thing, for all that we have is but by God's hand.

GLEANINGS FROM THE BOOK OF 2 CHRONICLES

2 Chronicles 1:10 *Give me now wisdom and knowledge, that I may go out and come in before this people: for who can judge this thy people, that is so great?*

"GIVE ME NOW WISDOM AND KNOWLEDGE"

Of all the things Solomon could have asked the Lord for, he simply asked for wisdom and knowledge! We would do well to ask and seek after the same thing! Let us pray even today for wisdom in our daily walk and the knowledge to accomplish what needs to be accomplished!

---

2 Chronicles 6:1 *Then said Solomon, The LORD hath said that he would dwell in the thick darkness.*

"THAT HE WOULD DWELL IN THE THICK DARKNESS"

WOW! I am reminded of lyrics that say, "GOD WALKS THE DARK HILLS!" The Psalmist wrote, Though I walk through the valley of the shadow of death, I will fear no evil." No matter how dark the trial or dim the days ahead, know this...THE LORD HATH SAID THAT HE WOULD DWELL IN THE THICK DARKNESS!

---

2 Chronicles 6:18 *But will God in very deed dwell with men on the earth? behold, heaven and the heaven of heavens cannot contain thee; how much less this house which I have built!*

"BEHOLD, HEAVEN AND THE HEAVEN OF HEAVENS CANNOT CONTAIN THEE"

In our wildest imagination, we cannot for a moment even begin to comprehend the greatness of our God! Solomon declared that all of Heaven and the Heaven of Heavens could not contain Him! Our God truly is an awesome God!

2 Chronicles 12:7 *And when the LORD saw that they humbled themselves, the word of the LORD came to Shemaiah, saying, They have humbled themselves; therefore I will not destroy them, but I will grant them some deliverance; and my wrath shall not be poured out upon Jerusalem by the hand of Shishak.*

"AND WHEN THE LORD SAW THAT THEY HUMBLED THEMSELVES"

Whether or not God passes judgment on a nation is determined by that nation's humility. When Israel humbled herself, then God had mercy, but when Israel did that which they thought was right in their own eyes, God passed judgment. The ideology in America today that says, "I can do whatever I please," is not scriptural. America must humble herself; if she won't do it on her own, God will.

2 Chronicles 13:18 *Thus the children of Israel were brought under at that time, and the children of Judah prevailed, because they relied upon the LORD God of their fathers.*

"AND THE CHILDREN OF JUDAH PREVAILED, BECAUSE THEY RELIED UPON THE LORD GOD OF THEIR FATHERS"

Every good success story starts with a good foundation! Judah's success was due to their reliance on the LORD! Do you want to succeed today? Whom do you rely on?

2 Chronicles 16:9 *For the eyes of the LORD run to and fro throughout the whole earth, to shew himself strong in the behalf of them whose heart is perfect toward him. Herein thou hast done foolishly: therefore from henceforth thou shalt have wars.*

"FOR THE EYES OF THE LORD RUN TO AND FRO THROUGHOUT THE WHOLE EARTH"

The Creator of Heaven and Earth sees all and knows all! Everything that you do and say today, God is watching! Let all that we do be acceptable in His sight!

---

2 Chronicles 20:10 *Now it is in mine heart to make a covenant with the LORD God of Israel, that his fierce wrath may turn away from us.*

"NOW IT IS IN MINE HEART TO MAKE A COVENANT WITH THE LORD GOD"

What is in our hearts this morning? Are we focused on what we should be or does something else occupy our hearts and minds? Is it in our hearts to seek THE LORD GOD?

---

2 Chronicles 21:20 *Thirty and two years old was he when he began to reign, and he reigned in Jerusalem eight years, and departed without being desired. Howbeit they buried him in the city of David, but not in the sepulchres of the kings.*

"AND DEPARTED WITHOUT BEING DESIRED"

Jehoram was a king so evil that God plagued him with a sickness so severe his bowels fell out. His sin was so abhorrent in the eyes of God that God made him abhorrent in the eyes of people. Even though he was a king there was no honoring of him upon his death. Sin is only fun for a season; then all must face the consequences!

---

2 Chronicles 26:5 *And he sought God in the days of Zechariah, who had understanding in the visions of God: and as long as he sought the LORD, God made him to prosper.*

"AND AS LONG AS HE SOUGHT THE LORD, GOD MADE HIM TO PROSPER"

God's promises are true! He will certainly bless those who are faithful and serve Him! Prosper does not always mean wealth and riches but success in our everyday endeavors or just overcoming a burdensome task! Whatever it may be, know this: He will take care of His own!

---

2 Chronicles 32:8 *With him is an arm of flesh; but with us is the LORD our God to help us, and to fight our battles. And the people rested themselves upon the words of Hezekiah king of Judah.*

"WITH HIM IS AN ARM OF FLESH; BUT WITH US IS THE LORD OUR GOD TO HELP US"

The king of Assyria made a bold statement towards King Hezekiah. He stated that no other gods had defeated him. Hezekiah proclaimed that their God was not just any god but "THE LORD OUR GOD," and He is greater than the arm of flesh! Be of good courage today, for greater is He that dwells within us then that which is in the world!

---

2 Chronicles 34:2 *And he did that which was right in the sight of the LORD, and walked in the ways of David his father, and declined neither to the right hand, nor to the left.*

"AND DECLINED NEITHER TO THE RIGHT HAND, NOR TO THE LEFT"

There seems to be a thought process that says, "It's only wrong if you go too far to the left." Multiple times in scripture, we see this ideology that states to go neither too far right or too far left. Though true, liberalism can be a dangerous thing and yet so can be a dogmatic legalistic attitude! We should be as narrow-minded as the Word of God is, neither too far right or too far left!

---

2 Chronicles 36:23 *Thus saith Cyrus king of Persia, All the kingdoms of the earth hath the LORD God of heaven given me; and he hath charged me to build him an house in Jerusalem, which is in Judah. Who is there among you of all his people? The LORD his God be with him, and let him go up.*

"WHO IS THERE AMONG YOU OF ALL HIS PEOPLE"

Who is there among you that will go up and do the work? Finding young men willing to do the work of the Lord is a rare thing; but rather, many a young man will seek a paycheck first and then serve.

GLEANINGS FROM THE BOOK OF EZRA

Ezra 3:11 *And they sang together by course in praising and giving thanks unto the LORD; because he is good, for his mercy endureth for ever toward Israel. And all the people shouted with a great shout, when they praised the LORD, because the foundation of the house of the LORD was laid.*

"AND ALL THE PEOPLE SHOUTED WITH A GREAT SHOUT, WHEN THEY PRAISED THE LORD, BECAUSE THE FOUNDATION OF THE HOUSE OF THE LORD WAS LAID"

There was great excitement among God's people when the foundation was laid for the rebuilding of the temple. The excitement was so great that it was heard and made known throughout the land! Are you excited about the things of God? The excitement was simply over the foundation of the temple. We today have so much more to be excited about, and yet we remain silent!

Ezra 4:12 *Be it known unto the king, that the Jews which came up from thee to us are come unto Jerusalem, building the rebellious and the bad city, and have set up the walls thereof, and joined the foundations.*

"BUILDING THE REBELLIOUS AND THE BAD CITY"

Ezra and his companions were met with resistance by those who wrote letters to the king of Persia. These letters stated that those that were rebuilding the temple and the city of Jerusalem were rebellious. If doing the Lord's work is a rebellious work, then label me a rebel.

Ezra 9:6 *And said, O my God, I am ashamed and blush to lift up my face to thee, my God: for our iniquities are increased over our head, and our trespass is grown up unto the heavens.*

"I AM ASHAMED AND BLUSH TO LIFT UP MY FACE TO THEE"

I wonder: if we were really truly honest with ourselves, how many of us would like Ezra cry out… "I am ashamed and blush to lift up my face to thee!"

GLEANINGS FROM THE BOOK OF NEHEMIAH

Nehemiah 4:6 *So built we the wall; and all the wall was joined together unto the half thereof: for the people had a mind to work.*

"FOR THE PEOPLE HAD A MIND TO WORK"

What a great thing it is when God's people have a mind to work! The key ingredient in the success of any ministry is a good work ethic! No matter the task, just attack it with vigor one stone at a time. Things get done when there is a mind to work!
Half the battle in regard to getting things done is the mindset. What may seem impossible or to hard is often nothing more than our mind telling us that we can't; and yet, is anything too hard for God? I can do all things through Christ which strengtheneth me. If but God's people had a mind to work.

Nehemiah 6:11 *And I said, Should such a man as I flee? and who is there, that, being as I am, would go into the temple to save his life? I will not go in.*

"AND I SAID, SHOULD SUCH A MAN AS I FLEE"

Should a man of God flee? Nehemiah would not. The position of a pastor is often portrayed as weak and frail. On the contrary; a man of God ought to be the voice of leadership and guidance. Leaders are not weak nor frail.

Nehemiah 13:2 *Because they met not the children of Israel with bread and with water, but hired Balaam against them, that he should curse them: howbeit our God turned the curse into a blessing.*

"GOD TURNED THE CURSE INTO A BLESSING"

How quickly we forget the God of our salvation when our enemies come against us. When they curse us and mean us harm, we must remember that God is in control and that He can surely turn cursing into blessing!

GLEANINGS FROM THE BOOK OF ESTHER

Esther 4:14 *For if thou altogether holdest thy peace at this time, then shall there enlargement and deliverance arise to the Jews from another place; but thou and thy father's house shall be destroyed: and who knoweth whether thou art come to the kingdom for such a time as this?*

"FOR IF THOU ALTOGETHER HOLDEST THY PEACE AT THIS TIME"

If God's people remain silent, then people will die. How relevant this statement is even today. We remain silent in our prayers as well as in our politics. "If my people, which are called by name, will humble themselves, and pray…" It is in such times as these that we need desperately to seek God's face in prayer, and we need not be silent in regard to our leaders both locally and nationally.

Esther 8:11 *Wherein the king granted the Jews which were in every city to gather themselves together, and to stand for their life, to destroy, to slay, and to cause to perish, all the power of the people and province that would assault them, both little ones and women, and to take the spoil of them for a prey,*

"AND TO STAND FOR THEIR LIFE"

As I am writing this, just twenty-four hours earlier, an armed gunman walked into a Sunday morning church service in White Settlement, Texas, with the intent to kill. As he opened fire, a church member fired back with the weapon he was carrying. Though the gunman killed one individual, a law abiding citizen took a stand against his evil actions and prevented what may have been a horrific massacre! The Jews were given the authority to stand up for their lives in the book of Esther! There comes a time when the righteous must take a stand against those that would seek out to harm or do evil against the innocent!

GLEANINGS FROM THE BOOK OF JOB

Job 1:9 *Then Satan answered the LORD, and said, Doth Job fear God for nought?*

"DOTH JOB FEAR GOD FOR NOUGHT"

What a great question! Why do you serve God? What is the basis of your fear of God? Is there any fear of God at all? What drives you to go to church, to read your Bible, or to pray! Either you truly believe that God is who His Word says He is, or you don't! A true Christian will fear his LORD, and his life will reflect it!

Job 2:9 *Then said his wife unto him, Dost thou still retain thine integrity? curse God, and die.*

"DOST THOU STILL RETAIN THINE INTEGRITY"

Interesting that after all that had happened to Job, his wife made this statement, "DOST THOU STILL RETAIN THY INTEGRITY?" I believe a true Christian, even in the face of adversity, can still retain their INTEGRITY! On this day, let us not forget Whom we serve and Who is in control!

Job 4:8 *Even as I have seen, they that plow iniquity, and sow wickedness, reap the same.*

"THEY THAT PLOW INIQUITY, AND SOW WICKEDNESS, REAP THE SAME"

It is a true statement you reap what you sow; if you plant a seed of wickedness, it is just that which will grow, for your sin shall find you out! What you dish out will come back to you in full force!

Job 7:1 *Is there not an appointed time to man upon earth? are not his days also like the days of an hireling?*

"IS THERE NOT AN APPOINTED TIME TO MAN UPON EARTH"

We all have an appointment with death. Until that time comes, we also have a job to do. Is it not good to know that it is only temporary employment? Like a hireling who is employed to do a specific task and, once that task is complete, is then relieved of his labor.

Job 9:22 *This is one thing, therefore I said it, He destroyeth the perfect and the wicked.*

"HE DESTROYETH THE PERFECT AND THE WICKED"

Why do bad things happen to Godly people? The simple answer is that God's people live in an evil world. As a matter of fact, evil is more apt to go after the Godly than the ungodly. Why does God not intervene? If God simply laid out a bed of roses for us, we would not have any need of a Savior much less desire a relationship with Him.

Job 11:14 *If iniquity be in thine hand, put it far away, and let not wickedness dwell in thy tabernacles.*

"AND LET NOT WICKEDNESS DWELL IN THY TABERNACLES"

Could it be time for some spring cleaning?

Job 12:22 *He discovereth deep things out of darkness, and bringeth out to light the shadow of death.*

"HE DISCOVERETH DEEP THINGS OUT OF DARKNESS"

When things seem so dark and the world seems to be spinning out of control, God can see things that we can't! He discovereth deep things out of darkness! He alone can give you the wisdom you need in your darkest hour!

Job 16:4 *I also could speak as ye do: if your soul were in my soul's stead, I could heap up words against you, and shake mine head at you.*

"IF YOUR SOUL WERE IN MY SOUL'S STEAD"

It is easy for someone to make comments from the other side of the fence. Until you walk a mile in another man's shoes, you truly do not have any idea of another's trial or pain. Commentary is not always needed; but rather, a shoulder to lean on and a prayer on behalf of the one suffering is often more applicable.

Job 16:21 *O that one might plead for a man with God, as a man pleadeth for his neighbour!*

"O THAT ONE MIGHT PLEAD FOR A MAN WITH GOD"

Too often, our prayers are laced with extravagant and flowery wording. We are to talk to God as we would talk to a friend, more so in a time of need. Trying to impress God with a manicured speech is not what He wants to hear from us!

Job 29:6 *When I washed my steps with butter, and the rock poured me out rivers of oil;*

"WHEN I WASHED MY STEPS WITH BUTTER"

Job, in the midst of his trial, reflects on a time when he would wash his feet with milk and butter. The average person would simply rinse with water. Job reflects on how good God had been to him in the past. On this Memorial Day here in America, let us not forget that God has truly blessed this country. Compared to other places in the world, living in the United States is like butter between your toes. Let us not forget those that have given their lives so that we might enjoy the fruits of their sacrifice.

Job 31:1 *I made a covenant with mine eyes; why then should I think upon a maid?*

"I MADE A COVENANT WITH MINE EYES"

Many a man has fallen by what he has viewed with his eyes. Women are subject to this as well, but so much more the man. It would serve a man well to make a covenant with his eyes!

Job 31:4 *Doth not he see my ways, and count all my steps?*

"DOTH NOT HE SEE MY WAYS, AND COUNT ALL MY STEPS"

God not only sees all that we do but the process we take to get there. There is a difference between one who is drawn into sin and one who intentionally sins for one's selfish reasons! He counts our steps! He takes note of the intent of the heart! It could be that we need to backstep on some things today!

Job 32:9 *Great men are not always wise: neither do the aged understand judgment.*

"GREAT MEN ARE NOT ALWAYS WISE"

One of the great failures of a man of God is to not seek counsel. More specifically, to ignore the counsel of a younger man. It goes without saying that the younger ought to respect and seek wisdom from the elder, but a wise man becomes a fool when he thinks he has nothing else to learn!
A man's high position does not make him wise. Even the aged can learn from the young. We will not know all things until we see Christ. There is always something to learn and understanding to be had until we take our final breath.

Job 37:5 *God thundereth marvellously with his voice; great things doeth he, which we cannot comprehend.*

"WHICH WE CANNOT COMPREHEND"

Who can tame the thunder or contain it in a box? If we would but take a moment and observe just how marvelous His wonders are, then we might just understand that He is capable of also caring for us!

Job 42:2 *I know that thou canst do everything, and that no thought can be withholden from thee.*

"AND THAT NO THOUGHT CAN BE WITHHOLDEN FROM THEE"

Not even our thoughts are secret from God. It may not come forth out of your mouth, but God will certainly hold us accountable for each and every thought, whether it be good or evil!

Job 42:10 *And the LORD turned the captivity of Job, when he prayed for his friends: also the LORD gave Job twice as much as he had before.*

"WHEN HE PRAYED FOR HIS FRIENDS"

Interesting that Job's sorrow and troubles did not turn around until he began to focus on others and not himself! The Lord turned the captivity of Job when he prayed for his friends. If you want to change your circumstance, begin by praying for others!

GLEANINGS FROM THE BOOK OF PSALMS

Psalm 9:12 *When he maketh inquisition for blood, he remembereth them: he forgetteth not the cry of the humble.*

"WHEN HE MAKETH INQUISITION FOR BLOOD"

From those who have been violently murdered to the simple cry of the humble, God not only hears their cry, but He does not forget those that come against God's people. God will avenge His own.

Psalm 11:3 *If the foundations be destroyed, what can the righteous do?*

"WHAT CAN THE RIGHTEOUS DO"

In days like these, what can the righteous do? In verse one of this very same chapter, we find the answer in the Psalmist's words: "In the Lord put I my trust..." and in verse seven: "For the righteous Lord loveth righteousness; his countenance doth behold the upright."

Psalm 14:2 *The LORD looked down from heaven upon the children of men, to see if there were any that did understand, and seek God.*

"TO SEE IF THERE WERE ANY THAT DID UNDERSTAND"

God looks down from Heaven and searches for those who are seeking Him and have understanding! God delights in those who study to show themselves approved of God, rightly dividing His Word of truth!

Psalm 22:20 *Deliver my soul from the sword; my darling from the power of the dog.*

"MY DARLING FROM THE POWER OF THE DOG"

Often called the Psalm of the cross. A prophetic and poetic glimpse at the pain and anguish our Savior would endure. Darling, meaning "that which is more precious than anything else." In this case the soul. Is there any singular thing more precious than the soul of a man? For what does it profit a man if he gain the whole world and yet lose his own soul?

Psalm 26:11 *But as for me, I will walk in mine integrity: redeem me, and be merciful unto me.*

"BUT AS FOR ME, I WILL WALK IN MINE INTEGRITY"

Many a Christian will declare one thing and yet live their lives with another standard! Let us live what we say! Let the child of God walk with integrity. Honest, upright, and righteous!

Psalm 26:12 *My foot standeth in an even place: in the congregations will I bless the LORD.*

"MY FOOT STANDETH IN AN EVEN PLACE"

An interesting statement considering one who would stand on uneven ground is subject to stumble and fall! As the old hymn reads...ON CHRIST THE SOLID ROCK I STAND, ALL OTHER GROUND IS SINKING SAND, ALL OTHER GROUND IS SINKING SAND!

Psalm 37:3 *Trust in the LORD, and do good; so shalt thou dwell in the land, and verily thou shalt be fed.*

"TRUST IN THE LORD"

No matter the circumstances around us, we are to trust in the Lord. It is His perfect will that we must seek. He will guide, protect and nourish those that are His own.

Psalm 37:25 *I have been young, and now am old; yet have I not seen the righteous forsaken, nor his seed begging bread.*

"YET HAVE I NOT SEEN THE RIGHTEOUS FORSAKEN"

Never anywhere or at any time has God ever forsaken the righteous! Not that we won't endure some trying times for so did the likes of Joseph and Job; "Yet have I not seen the righteous forsaken, nor his seed begging bread."

Psalm 39:1 *I said, I will take heed to my ways, that I sin not with my tongue: I will keep my mouth with a bridle, while the wicked is before me.*

"I WILL TAKE HEED TO MY WAYS, THAT I SIN NOT WITH MY TONGUE"

Good advice in this day and age of social media!

Psalm 51:10 *Create in me a clean heart, O God; and renew a right spirit within me.*

"AND RENEW A RIGHT SPIRIT WITHIN ME"

Create—as in the book of Genesis, when God created the heavens and the earth. The idea is to put something in us that was not there before. The purpose for this creation is to renew a right spirit, a spirit that will endure and be lasting through the ups and the downs of this life; for it is a broken and contrite spirit before God, one of humility and glorifying of God himself.

———————

Psalm 51:17 *The sacrifices of God are a broken spirit: a broken and a contrite heart, O God, thou wilt not despise.*

"THE SACRIFICES OF GOD ARE A BROKEN SPIRIT: A BROKEN AND A CONTRITE HEART"

More than sacrifice, ceremony, and ritual, God would much more desire a sweet and willing spirit and a broken heart ready to serve Him! What does not come from the heart is simply actions without sincerity! There are too many fake Christians simply going through the motions without true, heartfelt worship!

———————

Psalm 57:1 *Be merciful unto me, O God, be merciful unto me: for my soul trusteth in thee: yea, in the shadow of thy wings will I make my refuge, until these calamities be overpast.*

"IN THE SHADOW OF THY WINGS WILL I MAKE MY REFUGE"

Life is full of struggles and trials. It is a natural reaction to run to and lean on the ones we love. And yet, if we say we love God, why do we not cling to His Word? Let us not lean on our own understanding; but rather, let us hide in the shadow of His wings!

———————

Psalm 61:8 *So will I sing praise unto thy name for ever, that I may daily perform my vows.*

"SO I WILL SING PRAISE UNTO THY NAME FOR EVER"

Putting a song in your heart and a spring in your step will greatly help you to accomplish what needs to be done. Half the battle is just having the desire to get something accomplished. Knowing that God is our protection and keeper ought to be enough to put a smile on our faces.

Psalm 62:8 *Trust in him at all times; ye people, pour out your heart before him: God is a refuge for us. Selah.*

"TRUST IN HIM AT ALL TIMES"

Trust in Him at all times whether good times or bad. Believe that He is working all things for our good. Let us give of our whole heart even when it seems darkest, for it is in those times He becomes our refuge.

Psalm 62:11 *God hath spoken once; twice have I heard this; that power belongeth unto God.* **12** *Also unto thee, O Lord, belongeth mercy: for thou renderest to every man according to his work.*

"GOD HATH SPOKEN ONCE"

God spoke once, but David heard two things. First, David heard power in the voice of God; and second, David heard mercy. For as powerful as God is and able to defeat our enemies both physical and spiritual, He is likewise able to show mercy to those He loves.

Psalm 66:16 *Come and hear, all ye that fear God, and I will declare what he hath done for my soul.*

"AND I WILL DECLARE WHAT HE HATH DONE FOR MY SOUL"

There is no greater declaration than to be able to proclaim that one's soul has been saved from a devil's Hell!

Psalm 68:11 *The Lord gave the word: great was the company of those that published it.*

"THE LORD GAVE THE WORD"

The Word of God has not ceased its greatness; however, finding great men to publish it in today's day and time is another issue. The man who declares God's Word is certainly considered great in God's eyes!

Psalm 73:28 *But it is good for me to draw near to God: I have put my trust in the Lord GOD, that I may declare all thy works.*

"BUT IT IS GOOD FOR ME TO DRAW NEAR TO GOD"

There are many things that call to us on a daily basis. The things of this world are attractive to our flesh and call to us, and yet the best place to be is near God! Let us not allow the things of this life draw us away from where we really need to be, for "it is good for me to draw near to God!"

Psalm 77:3 *I remembered God, and was troubled: I complained, and my spirit was overwhelmed. Selah.*

"I REMEMBERD GOD"

Oh, that the child of God would seek Him on the mountain and not just in the valley. It is in our trial that we remember God. To say that we remember is to imply that we have forgotten. I'm glad He is there when we need Him most, but let us not forget that He, too, is the reason for those times we stand on mountain tops!

Psalm 81:7 *Thou calledst in trouble, and I delivered thee; I answered thee in the secret place of thunder: I proved thee at the waters of Meribah. Selah.*

"I ANSWERED THEE IN THE SECRET PLACE OF THUNDER"

God was a cloud by day and a fire by night to the children of Israel as the fled Egypt. To some, a thunderstorm is a terrible thing; but to others it is a wonderful thing. God answers our prayers sometimes in strange and miraculous ways. Sometimes, what may seem to be a terrible thing on the surface is but the hand of God working to our good.

Psalm 84:10 *For a day in thy courts is better than a thousand. I had rather be a doorkeeper in the house of my God, than to dwell in the tents of wickedness.*

"I HAD RATHER BE A DOORKEEPER IN THE HOUSE OF MY GOD, THAN TO DWELL IN THE TENTS OF WICKEDNESS"

The lowest of positions in the house of God is far greater than anything a wicked dwelling has to offer! Sin is only satisfying for a season, but the child of God has eternity to look forward to!

Psalm 90:12 *So teach us to number our days, that we may apply our hearts unto wisdom.*

"SO TEACH US TO NUMBER OUR DAYS"

Teach us to be aware of how short this life really is! Therefore, let us be mindful of the time and not pursue after foolishness but rather set our hearts after wisdom!

Psalm 91:1 *He that dwelleth in the secret place of the most High shall abide under the shadow of the Almighty.*

"HE THAT DWELLETH IN THE SECRET PLACE OF THE MOST HIGH"

A promise given to those who dwell in the secret place of God; or put a different way, the sacred place of the most High God. It is in the secret place we find peace and comfort in the shadow of His grace and mercy.

In other words, he whose habitation is in the Lord shall be under His shadow. The Christian who dwells with and around Godly things and Godly people have great peace that others do not have. God protects His own. Lord, hide me in Your secret place.

Psalm 101:2 *I will behave myself wisely in a perfect way. O when wilt thou come unto me? I will walk within my house with a perfect heart.*

"I WILL BEHAVE MYSELF WISELY IN A PERFECT WAY"

If there is any good wisdom for this day and time, it is that CHRISTIANS ought to seek wisdom and reflect on their behavior, especially when they are on FACEBOOK!

Psalm 103:8 *The LORD is merciful and gracious, slow to anger, and plenteous in mercy.*

"SLOW TO ANGER"

Of all the things I am thankful that my God is, the fact that He is slow to anger is the one I cherish most! How often and quickly we lose our temper over the silliest things! If God were to pour out His wrath on the things we do on a daily basis...well?

Psalm 106:20 *Thus they changed their glory into the similitude of an ox that eateth grass.*

"THUS THEY CHANGED THEIR GLORY"

The children of Israel forgot His great works and gave in to their own lusts and sin. Likewise, so changed their worship, for it also became tainted as well, trading the God of Heaven for a golden calf to be worshipped. We as God's people do not have the liberty to change the glory of God to justify our lustful desires.

They changed the character of God to an ox. They traded the glory of God for a golden ox. How many times in our lives have we traded the glory of God for fleshly and worldly desires?

Psalm 107:8 *Oh that men would praise the LORD for his goodness, and for his wonderful works to the children of men!*

"OH THAT MEN WOULD PRAISE THE LORD FOR HIS GOODNESS"

Oh, that we were more grateful for all that God has done for us! Oh, that we would take the time to just look around at all the many blessings God has bestowed upon us! Oh, that we would acknowledge His goodness and mercy! Our God is truly worthy of our praise!

Psalm 115:8 *They that make them are like unto them; so is every one that trusteth in them.*

"THEY THAT MAKE THEM ARE LIKE UNTO THEM"

The Biblical definition of dumb is clearly given. Idols have ears but cannot hear. They have eyes but cannot see. They have a mouth but cannot speak. The individual who goes and worships such an idol is no different. The worship of a graven image is as dumb as the image itself.

Psalm 118:24 *This is the day which the LORD hath made; we will rejoice and be glad in it.*

"THIS IS THE DAY WHICH THE LORD HATH MADE"

A verse that has been quoted relentlessly, and yet its context is often ignored. In verse twelve, it reads, "They compassed me about like bees..." The psalmist is aware of the attacks against him, and yet there is rejoicing. There is a confidence in knowing that God can destroy anyone or anything that stands in the way of His will. Therefore, let us rejoice, no matter the hardship of the day!

Psalm 119:9 *Wherewithal shall a young man cleanse his way? by taking heed thereto according to thy word.*

"BY TAKING HEED THERETO ACCORDING TO THY WORD"

Thy Word have I hid in my heart, that I might not sin against thee, oh Lord! What goes in is what will flow out! The cleanliness of one's life is determined by the washing of the Word of God!

Psalm 122:1 *I was glad when they said unto me, Let us go into the house of the LORD.*

"I WAS GLAD WHEN THEY SAID UNTO ME"

During a time of unrest in Israel and in Jerusalem, the Psalmist rejoices to come into the house of the Lord. If there is a place to find answers and peace during these days of unrest, it is truly the house of the Lord!

Psalm 124:2 *If it had not been the LORD who was on our side, when men rose up against us: 3 Then they had swallowed us up quick, when their wrath was kindled against us:*

"IF IT HAD NOT BEEN THE LORD"

Take a moment to look around you at all that the Lord has provided! All the many blessings He has given! If it had not been the Lord, then who?

―――――――――――――――

Psalm 124:8 *Our help is in the name of the LORD, who made heaven and earth.*

"OUR HELP IS IN THE NAME OF THE LORD"

At the name of Jesus, demons must flee! How mighty is our God that we find insurmountable strength in but only His name!

―――――――――――――――

Psalm 132:3 *I will not give sleep to mine eyes, or slumber to mine eyelids, 4 Until I find out a place for the LORD, an habitation for the mighty God of Jacob.*

"UNTIL I FIND OUT A PLACE FOR THE LORD"

The day is full of doings and going here and there. Too often, we end the day in exhaustion; and yet amongst our busy schedule, we have not included the Lord. The Lord should be included in every aspect of our daily routine. Let us not forget at the end of the day to thank the Lord for the blessings of the day!

When Jesus was in the garden of Gethsemane, He questioned His disciples as to why they could not watch and pray one hour. And yet many go through their entire day without finding time for the Lord.

―――――――――――――――

Psalm 133:1 *Behold how good and how pleasant it is: for brethren to dwell together in unity!*

"FOR BRETHREN TO DWELL TOGETHER IN UNITY"

Dysfunction and disorder are not something God approves of. For there in God's house, worship is removed and replaced with disorder! When brothers and sisters in Christ get along, there is a sweet spirit and environment conducive for God to meet with us!

Psalm 139:17 *How precious also are thy thoughts unto me, O God! how great is the sum of them!*

"HOW PRECIOUS ALSO ARE THY THOUGHTS UNTO ME"

Precious are the thoughts toward us from the God of Heaven. Put another way, sincere are His thoughts towards His children. Thoughts not in jest but rather with promise. God will back up His thoughts with actions.

Psalm 142:4 *I looked on my right hand, and beheld, but there was no man that would know me: refuge failed me; no man cared for my soul.*

"NO MAN CARED FOR MY SOUL"

Generally speaking, the world does not care if you live or die. Like a vapor, we are here today and gone tomorrow. It is the breath of God that makes man a living soul. Therefore, what is God's is His concern. Man in general does not care about your soul. If we as Christians care about what God thinks, then we should care about the fate of a man's soul

---

Psalm 145:3 *Great is the LORD, and greatly to be praised; and his greatness is unsearchable.*

"AND HIS GREATNESS IS UNSEARCHABLE"

Just as God has no beginning and no end, so are His actions! An attempt to seek out God's limits is but futile, for His greatness has no beginning and no end! Let us proclaim how great is our God!

GLEANINGS FROM THE BOOK OF PROVERBS

Proverbs 1:7 *The fear of the LORD is the beginning of knowledge: but fools despise wisdom and instruction.*

"THE FEAR OF THE LORD IS THE BEGINNING OF KNOWLEDGE"

One does not simply gain knowledge through education. The knowledge that is spoken of here is not something that man can supply; but rather, it is a Godliness and discernment of right or wrong. To know right from wrong, one must first revere God in fear and trembling.

Proverbs 3:3 *Let not mercy and truth forsake thee: bind them about thy neck; write them upon the table of thine heart:*

"LET NOT MERCY AND TRUTH FORSAKE THEE"

Like a necklace around the neck as a constant reminder. Let us always be aware of the mercy and truth of God! Let us apply the Word of God to our hearts insomuch that in whatever our situation, we might draw from wisdom.

Proverbs 4:26 *Ponder the path of thy feet, and let all thy ways be established.*

"PONDER THE PATH OF THY FEET"

Think before you act. Too often, actions are taken without any thought of the consequences. In the very next chapter, the lips of a strange woman are smooth compared to her end, which is bitter and sharp like a two-edged sword. Likewise, so is the wisdom of Scripture a two-edged sword. Both will cut you to the heart, but one will leave your life in ruin while the other will reward you with grace and mercy.

Proverbs 5:23 *He shall die without instruction; and in the greatness of his folly he shall go astray.*

"HE SHALL DIE WITHOUT INSTRUCTION"

I can't help but think that many a man has died needlessly and way too young. Wasted before his time. Why? Either he was not taught, or he refused to listen to sound wisdom.

Proverbs 6:19 *A false witness that speaketh lies, and he that soweth discord among brethren.*

"HE THAT SOWETH DISCORD AMONG THE BRETHREN"

Too often, we point out the abominations of others while overlooking our own. Proverbs calls a froward mouth naughty. This person is all talk and no actions, mischievous, and one who sows discord among the brethren. Ironically, the context of this passage has to do with laziness. It would do many a Christian well to find something better to do than to talk down about others.

Proverbs 8:35 *For whoso findeth me findeth life, and shall obtain favour of the LORD.* **36** *But he that sinneth against me wrongeth his own soul: all they that hate me love death.*

"ALL THEY THAT HATE ME LOVE DEATH"

A comparison of good and bad wisdom. The rejection of truth, knowledge, and good wisdom is likened unto the man who gives up everything for one night of pleasure with a whorish woman. It is foolish and destructive; therefore, he is a lover of death!

Proverbs 12:15 *The way of a fool is right in his own eyes: but he that hearkeneth unto counsel is wise.*

"BUT HE THAT HEARKENETH UNTO COUNSEL IS WISE"

It is a foolish thing to not adhere to good counsel. For someone to ignore wisdom to do that which seems right in their own eyes, surely it will not end well. It is a good thing to listen before we react!

Proverbs 15:16 *Better is little with the fear of the LORD than great treasure and trouble therewith.*

"BETTER IS LITTLE WITH THE FEAR OF THE LORD"

It is better to have little to nothing and walk with God than to have numerous wealth and riches and be lost. The poor man in Christ shall inherit streets of gold, but the lost man will take nothing with him to Hell.

Proverbs 16:4 *The LORD hath made all things for himself: yea, even the wicked for the day of evil.*

"THE LORD HATH MADE ALL THINGS FOR HIMSELF"

There are no mistakes with God, for even that which is evil serves a purpose in His ultimate plan. Joseph's brothers meant him evil, but God used those circumstances to elevate Joseph. Even today, the things we don't understand are but small pieces in the big puzzle of God's plan.

Proverbs 17:19 *He loveth transgression that loveth strife: and he that exalteth his gate seeketh destruction.*

"AND HE THAT EXALTETH HIS GATE SEEKETH DESTRUCTION"

God promotes and lifts up leaders. The man who exalts himself will surely see destruction.

Proverbs 20:17 *Bread of deceit is sweet to a man; but afterwards his mouth shall be filled with gravel.*

"BUT AFTERWARDS HIS MOUTH SHALL BE FILLED WITH GRAVEL"

Sin is only fun for a season. Everything we do has a consequence, whether it be good or bad. Gain by false pretenses is sweet for the moment, but the consequences of such actions are as if you were chewing on rocks. When gain comes from the hand of God, it is sweet to the tongue indeed.

Proverbs 21:31 *The horse is prepared against the day of battle: but safety is of the LORD.*

"BUT SAFETY IS OF THE LORD"

All the preparation in the world cannot keep you from harm. The One who holds you in His hands is the One who protects. Our faith and trust are not in the things of this earth, but rather in the Creator of all things. Though it is good to prepare, our safety, however, is of the Lord.

Proverbs 25:2 *It is the glory of God to conceal a thing: but the honour of kings is to search out a matter.*

"THE HONOUR OF KINGS IS TO SEARCH OUT A MATTER"

Patience is a virtue. Taking the time to research and gain all the facts is a character trait worthy of kings. Leaders research and study before they react.

Proverbs 27:20 *Hell and destruction are never full; so the eyes of man are never satisfied.*

"HELL AND DESTRUCTION ARE NEVER FULL"

The seeking of wealth and riches can consume a man. Such actions can destroy a man. Such actions have sent many to a devil's Hell. Anything that comes before God is idolatry. Hell and destruction are never full, and yet one must have a reservation to enter Heaven.

Proverbs 30:5 *Every word of God is pure: he is a shield unto them that put their trust in him. 6 Add thou not unto his words, lest he reprove thee, and thou be found a liar.*

"ADD THOU NOT UNTO HIS WORDS"

The importance of not changing the Word of God in any way, shape, or form is followed with a warning! Be careful; for if you do, God will reprove thee, and you will be declared a liar by God Himself! His word is pure; therefore, to change any portion of His Word is to taint it.

GLEANINGS FROM THE BOOK OF ECCLESIASTES

Ecclesiastes 2:14 *The wise man's eyes are in his head; but the fool walketh in darkness: and I myself perceived also that one event happeneth to them all.*

"THAT ONE EVENT HAPPENETH TO THEM ALL"

"All is vanity" is the message of Ecclesiastes. Even righteousness is in vain. In reality, it doesn't matter how you live because, in the end, we all die. Though it's good to live a righteous life, it is all for nothing without Christ. Good will not get you into heaven. We are righteous through Christ, but our own righteousness is but filthy rags.

Ecclesiastes 4:6 *Better is an handful with quietness, than both the hands full with travail and vexation of spirit.*

"BETTER IS A HANDFUL WITH QUIETNESS"

It is better to have little and be content and happy than to have great riches and not be content. The man who cannot be content will never find joy. True joy comes from the Lord, thus, the man without Christ is most miserable.

Ecclesiastes 5:10 *He that loveth silver shall not be satisfied with silver; nor he that loveth abundance with increase: this is also vanity.*

"HE THAT LOVETH SILVER SHALL NOT BE SATISFIED WITH SILVER"

Truly, the love of money is the root of all evil. Success is not a bad thing in and of itself. The greater question is, what drives you to be successful? If it is but for gain, you will never find true peace and happiness. If it is to the glory of God, then success is sweet!

Ecclesiastes 5:20 *For he shall not much remember the days of his life; because God answereth him in the joy of his heart.*

"FOR HE SHALL NOT MUCH REMEMBER THE DAYS OF HIS LIFE"

Man will remember very little of the hardships of this life when his focus is on the goodness of God. If one would simply focus on others, they would not be focused on themselves. It is a reasonable and sensible concept. Man will not complain if his heart is full of the joy of the Lord.

Ecclesiastes 9:10 *Whatsoever thy hand findeth to do, do it with thy might; for there is no work, nor device, nor knowledge, nor wisdom, in the grave, whither thou goest.*

"WHATSOEVER THY HAND FINDETH TO DO, DO IT WITH THY MIGHT"

Life is but a vapor, we are here today and gone tomorrow. Whatever the task, do it to the best of your ability. More important than daily tasks though, is for us to understand that time is short to apply wisdom. Wisdom is the Word of God. Death is too late. The rich man cried from hell for help, but it was too late. Let us redeem the time, for we know not what the day holds.

GLEANINGS FROM THE BOOK OF SONG OF SOLOMON

Song of Solomon 2:4 *He brought me to the banqueting house, and his banner over me was love.*

"AND HIS BANNER OVER ME WAS LOVE"

When a soldier would sit at a kings table, his in insignia would be displayed behind him. So we as the bride of Christ will one day feast at His table, and Christ's banner with His insignia will be displayed over us. Our Lord fought the battle over sin on the cross, and He did so out of love for you and for me. His insignia is one of love!

Consider for a moment a banquet hall fit for a king, lavishly decorated in gold and precious jewels. All of the king's men and advisors have gathered together for the feast and eagerly await the announcement of whom the king declares his love to. Through the door comes a dirty, smelly, greasy haired, bruised, scabby, and sunburnt girl into the banquet hall. The king sits her down under a banner that says, "I love her." Such is the King of Kings' and Lord of Lords' love for us. For God so loved the world!

Song of Solomon 2:16 *My beloved is mine, and I am his: he feedeth among the lilies.*

"MY BELOVED IS MINE, AND I AM HIS"

The book of Song of Solomon is the lovely picture of Christ's love for the church and the church's love for Christ. Do we ever just stop to consider the One who spoke this world into existence, the Great Physician, the One who laid down His life that we might live. I can arise every morning and proclaim...I AM HIS AND HE IS MINE!

Song of Solomon 6:3 *I am my beloved's, and my beloved is mine: he feedeth among the lilies.*

"I AM MY BELOVED'S, AND MY BELOVED IS MINE"

The theme of the book of Song of Solomon is "pure love" and the pureness of Christ's love for His Church. I belong to Jesus, and He belongs to me! There has never been a greater or purer expression of love than that of our Savior giving His life for our sins.

GLEANINGS FROM THE BOOK OF ISAIAH

Isaiah 1:1 *The vision of Isaiah the son of Amoz, which he saw concerning Judah and Jerusalem in the days of Uzziah, Jotham, Ahaz, and Hezekiah, kings of Judah.*

"THE VISION OF ISAIAH THE SON OF AMOZ"

Isaiah never lost his vision for the things of God, no matter who was on the throne. Uzziah was a prideful king, Jotham was a goodly king but avoided the house of the Lord, Ahaz was an ungodly king who committed criminal acts, and Hezekiah was a godly king living by faith and trusting God for deliverance from his enemies. Through good kings and bad kings, Isaiah never lost his vision. Likewise, neither should we; for the God on the mountain is the God in the valley, and the God of the good times is still God in the bad.

Isaiah 3:8 *For Jerusalem is ruined, and Judah is fallen: because their tongue and their doings are against the LORD, to provoke the eyes of his glory.*

"FOR JERUSALEM IS RUINED, AND JUDAH IS FALLEN"

Why? Because of their tongue and their doings. A nation that will denounce the God of creation and choose a vile and repulsive life of sin over righteousness will certainly result in ruin. A nation's fall and ruin is of their own making. The only way to avoid such ruin is for a nation's heart to turn back to God.

Isaiah 3:10 *Say ye to the righteous, that it shall be well with him: for they shall eat the fruit of their doings.*

"FOR THEY SHALL EAT THE FRUIT OF THEIR DOINGS"

For the just shall live by faith, and you reap what you sow. The strength of a Christian is the power behind that which he sows. God will take care of His own; we are to simply work faithfully in His fields. God will provide for the needs of His people.

Isaiah 6:4 *And the posts of the door moved at the voice of him that cried, and the house was filled with smoke.*

"AND THE POSTS OF THE DOOR MOVED AT THE VOICE OF HIM THAT CRIED"

The very voice of God can shake the foundation of Heaven. Imagine, for just a moment, if God would command the destruction of a nation! It was at God's command that fire and brimstone rained on Sodom and Gomorrah.

Isaiah 8:9 *Associate yourselves, O ye people, and ye shall be broken in pieces; and give ear, all ye of far countries: gird yourselves, and ye shall be broken in pieces; gird yourselves, and ye shall be broken in pieces.*

"ASSOCIATE YOURSELVES, O YE PEOPLE, AND YE SHALL BE BROKEN IN PIECES"

It is said that you are lucky if you have one true friend in life. Too often, the people that we call friends are nothing more than associations. We often rely on those associations for help in our time of need only to find disappointment. Jesus is a friend who sticks closer than a brother. Let us be careful of whom we trust with the cares of this life.

Isaiah 11:9 *They shall not hurt nor destroy in all my holy mountain: for the earth shall be full of the knowledge of the LORD, as the waters cover the sea.*

"FOR THE EARTH SHALL BE FULL OF THE KNOWLEDGE OF THE LORD"

When Christ shall come and once again restore His kingdom, then righteousness shall prevail. The lion will lay with the lamb, and there will be no division. The reason for such division is simply a lack of righteousness.

Isaiah 12:2 *Behold, God is my salvation; I will trust, and not be afraid: for the LORD JEHOVAH is my strength and my song; he also is become my salvation.*

"BEHOLD, GOD IS MY SALVATION"

For He is the author of my Salvation. It originates from God and God only. Salvation cannot be obtained by any other; therefore, we must put our trust in Him. He is our strength and our song! Let us sing praise for the God of our salvation!

Isaiah 12:3 *Therefore with joy shall ye draw water out of the wells of salvation.*

"DRAW WATER OUT OF THE WELLS OF SALVATION"

Be encouraged this morning, for the well of Salvation never dries up! His mercies are new every morning! No matter the circumstances this morning, you can face the day with JOY, because we have a well of SALVATION to draw from!
Too often, we try to attain joy from temporal things. Because those things break and/or rot and decay, our joy only last as long as those things are available. True and everlasting joy comes from trusting that Christ will protect us and secure us even into eternity.

Isaiah 21:6 *For thus hath the Lord said unto me, Go, set a watchman, let him declare what he seeth.*

"SET A WATCHMAN"

For thus hath the Lord said! We are to set a watchman, a lookout. Someone to take on the responsibility of looking out for danger and the approaching enemy. I fear that we have, as Christians, failed in the setting of watchmen in high places. The enemy seems to have infiltrated our houses of worship, our homes, and our hearts!

Isaiah 25:1 *O LORD, thou art my God; I will exalt thee, I will praise thy name; for thou hast done wonderful things; thy counsels of old are faithfulness and truth.*

"FOR THOU HAST DONE WONDERFUL THINGS"

Oh, that we would acknowledge how good the Lord truly is! Too often we focus on the negative and allow it to blur our vision. For every single negative, we could truly count hundreds of positive things the Lord has done! "Count your blessings, name them one by one; count your blessings, see what God hath done!"

Isaiah 25:1 *O LORD, thou art my God; I will exalt thee, I will praise thy name; for thou hast done wonderful things; thy counsels of old are faithfulness and truth.*

"I WILL PRAISE THY NAME; FOR THOU HAST DONE WONDERFUL THINGS"

The spans of time could not contain the wonderful things God has done. He is to be praised for His actions; He is to be praised for His counsels, for He is truly faithful and true.

Isaiah 26:3 *Thou wilt keep him in perfect peace, whose mind is stayed on thee: because he trusteth in thee.*

"THOU WILT KEEP HIM IN PERFECT PEACE"

There are two keys to having perfect peace in our lives. One is our mindset. We must have the mind of Christ. The Bible speaks of the renewing of one's mind. Second, we must trust Him, casting all our cares upon Him, for the just shall live by faith.

Stayed means detained or held. One who desires peace in a time of trouble must hold their attention on Christ. When he walked on water, Peter began to sink the moment he took his eyes of Jesus. When going through the struggles of this life, stay focused on Jesus.

Isaiah 28:1 *Woe to the crown of pride, to the drunkards of Ephraim, whose glorious beauty is a fading flower, which are on the head of the fat valleys of them that are overcome with wine!*

"WOE TO THE CROWN OF PRIDE, TO THE DRUNKARDS OF EPHRAIM"

Imagine a banquet table decorated with fine linen and glorious centerpieces of the freshest and most beautiful arrangements. The banquet hall is ordained with gold and most precious antiquities. The odors of food, flowers and sweet perfumes fill the air…and then someone vomits on the table, and another, and another! This is a picture of pride before destruction!

Isaiah 31:1 *Woe to them that go down to Egypt for help; and stay on horses, and trust in chariots, because they are many; and in horsemen, because they are very strong; but they look not unto the Holy One of Israel, neither seek the LORD!*

"WOE TO THEM THAT GO DOWN TO EGYPT FOR HELP"

It was Egypt that held them in bondage for so many years, and yet it was Egypt that they sought help from. Woe unto them that look to things for help that will ultimately leave them in bondage, such as addictions. Our help should come from the Lord. The thing that you seek help from could be the very thing that keeps you in bondage!

Isaiah 31:3 *Now the Egyptians are men, and not God; and their horses flesh, and not spirit. When the LORD shall stretch out his hand, both he that helpeth shall fall, and he that is holpen shall fall down, and they all shall fail together.*

"NOW THE EGYPTIANS ARE MEN, AND NOT GOD"

In a time when Egypt was known for its powerhouse military might, it did not compare to the power of our God! Men are men and God is still God! Nations rise and fall by His hand and His hand only!

Isaiah 32:17 *And the work of righteousness shall be peace; and the effect of righteousness quietness and assurance for ever.*

"AND THE WORK OF RIGHTEOUSNESS"

A recipe for the righteous. The work of the righteous is one of peace, and the effect of that peace is quietness and assurance. Not just a temporary assurance but an eternal assurance!

Isaiah 34:16 *Seek ye out of the book of the LORD, and read: no one of these shall fail, none shall want her mate: for my mouth it hath commanded, and his spirit it hath gathered them.*

"SEEK YE OUT OF THE BOOK OF THE LORD, AND READ"

Too often we look to the world for answers when we should be looking to the Lord! If its wisdom you seek, then open the Bible and seek wisdom in the pages of the Word of God. Read it daily, and daily you will grow in His grace and wisdom!

Isaiah 38:1 *In those days was Hezekiah sick unto death. And Isaiah the prophet the son of Amoz came unto him, and said unto him, Thus saith the LORD, Set thine house in order: for thou shalt die, and not live.*

"SET THINE HOUSE IN ORDER"

God is not the author of confusion. Scripture teaches very clearly that things ought to be done decently and in order. Hezekiah was told to put his house in order, for he was going to die. One thing is certain: we all have an appointment with death, though we know not the hour or day. It is important that we plan for that day. Is your physical house in order? Is your spiritual house in order?

Isaiah 38:5 *Go, and say to Hezekiah, Thus saith the LORD, the God of David thy father, I have heard thy prayer, I have seen thy tears: behold, I will add unto thy days fifteen years.*

"I HAVE SEEN THY TEARS"

Tears are the window to humility. We must come humbly before His throne of grace. Too often, our prayers are full of arrogance and self-righteousness. If we are to hear from Heaven then perhaps what is missing are the tears of humility, for "He that goeth forth and weepeth, bearing precious seed, shall doubtless come again with rejoicing, bringing his sheaves with him."

Isaiah 40:8 *The grass withereth, the flower fadeth: but the word of our God shall stand for ever.*

"BUT THE WORD OF OUR GOD SHALL STAND FOREVER"

After a week of letdowns, disappointments, sickness, and discouragement, what a joy to know that my hope is not in the things of this world! Though the things that surround me may falter, HIS WORD IS TRUE! "BUT THE WORD OF OUR GOD SHALL STAND FOREVER!"

Isaiah 40:28 *Hast thou not known? hast thou not heard, that the everlasting God, the LORD, the Creator of the ends of the earth, fainteth not, neither is weary? there is no searching of his understanding.*

"FAINTETH NOT, NEITHER IS WEARY"

The God of all creation, the Alpha and Omega, the beginning and the end, will not quit nor tire. God is in complete control and always has been and always will be, from start to finish.

Isaiah 43:1 *But now thus saith the LORD that created thee, O Jacob, and he that formed thee, O Israel, Fear not: for I have redeemed thee, I have called thee by thy name; thou art mine.*

"I HAVE CALLED THEE BY THY NAME"

Fear not, for God is calling your name. We live in a day and age of fear and anxiety. Israel had been left in ruin by war and were a nation in distress, but God called them by name and promised to do a new thing. Let us put fear aside and put our trust in God, for He and only He can do a new thing in our lives!

Isaiah 43:12 *I have declared, and have saved, and I have shewed, when there was no strange god among you: therefore ye are my witnesses, saith the LORD, that I am God.*

"THEREFORE YE ARE MY WITNESSES, SAITH THE LORD, THAT I AM GOD"

We have but one purpose on this earth, and that is but to proclaim to the world that He is GOD! Not just a god but that He is the one and only true God, and the only one that can save us from our sin!

Isaiah 43:19 *Behold, I will do a new thing; now it shall spring forth; shall ye not know it? I will even make a way in the wilderness, and rivers in the desert.*

"BEHOLD, I WILL DO A NEW THING"

The nation of Israel, in captivity in Babylon, is given the same promise as before when they were freed from Egypt. The application is relevant even today. It's been a rough year, and the church feels like it's being held captive, but God is ready to do a new thing this upcoming year!

Isaiah 45:22 *Look unto me, and be ye saved, all the ends of the earth: for I am God, and there is none else.*

"FOR I AM GOD, AND THERE IS NONE ELSE"

There is no other name under Heaven by which man might be saved! There is only one God and only one way to Heaven! For whosoever shall call upon the name of the Lord shall be saved!

Isaiah 48:10 *Behold, I have refined thee, but not with silver; I have chosen thee in the furnace of affliction.*

"I HAVE CHOSEN THEE IN THE FURNACE OF AFFLICTION"

Silver would be purged of its impurities seven times. Much like that process, the afflictions Israel must face are to purify them as a nation and draw them back to God. The application still holds true today. God still may afflict a nation in order to bring it to its knees.

Isaiah 50:1 *Thus saith the LORD, Where is the bill of your mother's divorcement, whom I have put away? or which of my creditors is it to whom I have sold you? Behold, for your iniquities have ye sold yourselves, and for your transgressions is your mother put away.*

"BEHOLD, FOR YOUR INIQUITIES HAVE YE SOLD YOURSELVES"

When things go wrong in our lives, we tend to blame God. In reality, God has nothing to do with the condition you find yourself in. Our state of living is a result of our sinful actions. We have no one to blame but ourselves.

Isaiah 52:7 *How beautiful upon the mountains are the feet of him that bringeth good tidings, that publisheth peace; that bringeth good tidings of good, that publisheth salvation; that saith unto Zion, Thy God reigneth!*

"HOW BEAUTIFUL UPON THE MOUNTAINS ARE THE FEET OF HIM THAT BRINGETH GOOD TIDINGS"

Can God declare your actions today a thing of beauty? Are they GOOD, PEACEFUL, OF GOOD REPORT, and most important..."THAT PUBLISH SALVATION!"

Isaiah 54:17 *No weapon that is formed against thee shall prosper; and every tongue that shall rise against thee in judgment thou shalt condemn. This is the heritage of the servants of the LORD, and their righteousness is of me, saith the LORD.*

"NO WEAPON THAT IS FORMED AGAINST THEE SHALL PROSPER"

The context must be in line with the previous verses. What God has determined to protect cannot be destroyed or torn down by any weapon or opposition from man. For God's ways are not man's ways, and His thoughts are not man's thoughts. If it is God's will, then nothing can stop it!

Isaiah 57:16 *For I will not contend for ever, neither will I be always wroth: for the spirit should fail before me, and the souls which I have made.*

"FOR I WILL NOT CONTEND FOR EVER"

The patience of God will not be held back forever. Grace and mercy will come to an end. His anger will only last so long, and this battle of good and evil will come to an end. The song lyric says, "He's coming back at midnight, and it's 11:59!"

Isaiah 59:1 *Behold, the LORD'S hand is not shortened, that it cannot save; neither his ear heavy, that it cannot hear:*

"THE LORD'S HAND IS NOT SHORTENED, THAT IT CANNOT SAVE"

No one is beyond His great and mighty arm. No one is so far gone that He cannot save! Nor is His ear ever so heavy from the cry of others that He does not hear us! He is always able and willing to hear us when we call!

Often, I've heard one say that God does not answer their prayers. And yet God hears every prayer that is prayed. His ear is always listening and never too heavy to hear us when we cry. It's not that God does not hear or answer; but rather, it is our actions that prohibit God from answering our prayer.

Isaiah 61:8 *For I the LORD love judgment, I hate robbery for burnt offering; and I will direct their work in truth, and I will make an everlasting covenant with them.*

"I HATE ROBBERY FOR BURNT OFFERING"

When the prophet Nathan approached David in regard to his sin with Bathsheba, he told a story of a man who was throwing a feast. He had multiple herds but stole a lamb to be sacrificed and eaten. In the same context, some are willing to give, but only if it is convenient or does not cost them anything.

Isaiah 61:10 *I will greatly rejoice in the LORD, my soul shall be joyful in my God; for he hath clothed me with the garments of salvation, he hath covered me with the robe of righteousness, as a bridegroom decketh himself with ornaments, and as a bride adorneth herself with her jewels.*

"I WILL GREATLY REJOICE IN THE LORD, MY SOUL SHALL BE JOYFUL IN MY GOD"

If you're a Christian, you have reason to rejoice! You have reason to be glad! Just as the bride and groom swell with excitement for the wedding day, so should we anticipate that day that we see Jesus!

GLEANINGS FROM THE BOOK OF JEREMIAH

Jeremiah 1:9 *Then the LORD put forth his hand, and touched my mouth. And the LORD said unto me, Behold, I have put my words in thy mouth.*

"BEHOLD, I HAVE PUT MY WORDS IN THY MOUTH"

God put His words in the mouth of Jeremiah. Too often, the man of God uses the pulpit for a soap box to promote his personal agenda. There is a message the world needs to hear. When we speak, let our words be God's words!

Jeremiah 3:1 *They say, If a man put away his wife, and she go from him, and become another man's, shall he return unto her again? shall not that land be greatly polluted? but thou hast played the harlot with many lovers; yet return again to me, saith the LORD.*

"BUT THOU HAST PLAYED THE HARLOT WITH MANY LOVERS"

Just as a spouse would take to the streets and have multiple intimate relationships and expect a warm return home and intimacy with their mate, so does God detest the whorish actions of His children in worldly and ungodly pleasures only to return to worship God as if nothing was wrong. Jeremiah sums it up in the final verse of this chapter when he says, "We lie down in our shame, and our confusion covereth us."

Jeremiah 4:19 *My bowels, my bowels! I am pained at my very heart; my heart maketh a noise in me; I cannot hold my peace, because thou hast heard, O my soul, the sound of the trumpet, the alarm of war.*

"I CANNOT HOLD MY PEACE, BECAUSE THOU HAST HEARD, O MY SOUL, THE SOUND OF THE TRUMPET, THE ALARM OF WAR"

As a Christian, you are faced with a decision, for we have heard the call to battle. A call that is one of the soul! As Joshua so boldly cried, "Choose you this day whom you will serve." The line has been drawn. Will you serve in the Lord's army, or will you retreat?

Jeremiah 5:1 *Run ye to and fro through the streets of Jerusalem, and see now, and know, and seek in the broad places thereof, if ye can find a man, if there be any that executeth judgment, that seeketh the truth; and I will pardon it.*

"IF YE CAN FIND A MAN"

This is the calling out of a nation and her long list of sins as well as a challenge to Jeremiah to search the streets and seek out honesty and truth, and yet, it would seem that there are none to be found. How long will a nation act in such a way before God will visit and deal with such ungodliness?

Jeremiah 5:25 *Your iniquities have turned away these things, and your sins have withholden good things from you.*

"AND YOUR SINS HAVE WITHHOLDEN GOOD THINGS FROM YOU"

The man that questions why God's blessings are not abundant in his life might want to evaluate his doings! Sin creates a barrier between God and His people, thus hindering the good things God has for us!

Jeremiah 6:15 *Were they ashamed when they had committed abomination? nay, they were not at all ashamed, neither could they blush: therefore they shall fall among them that fall: at the time that I visit them they shall be cast down, saith the LORD.*

"NEITHER COULD THEY BLUSH"

When a society reaches a point in which there is no shame and no one shows any remorse for their actions, we have truly reached the bottom and we are at risk of God's judgment. When people have traded blushing in for blatant sin, we can only expect the judgment of God to fall!

Jeremiah 8:14 *Why do we sit still? assemble yourselves, and let us enter into the defenced cities, and let us be silent there: for the LORD our God hath put us to silence, and given us water of gall to drink, because we have sinned against the LORD.*

"WHY DO WE SIT STILL"

After hearing the judgment of God, the people cried out, "Why do we sit still? Let us retreat to the defended cities and wait out this coming judgment in silence." This was not the reaction God was looking for; but rather, He was looking for a change of heart. Too often, we as Christians choose to hide away with our heads in the sand rather than to rise up and serve the Lord with boldness! Why do we sit still when we have sin to confess? Why do we sit still when there is judgment coming? Why do we sit still when there is a message to be shared with others?

Jeremiah 8:22 *Is there no balm in Gilead; is there no physician there? why then is not the health of the daughter of my people recovered?*

"IS THERE NO BALM IN GILIEAD"

The priests were often the physicians of the day. It was the priest who declared one clean or unclean in cases of leprosy. Just as the healing ointment is put on a wound, thus is the Word of God applied to a sin-sick soul! How sad when that spiritual healing cannot be found in the pulpit of a nation! Many a pulpit has become a place of comedy, politics, and storytelling. Thus, the cry is as relevant today as it was then, "Is there no balm in Gilead?"

Jeremiah 10:21 *For the pastors are become brutish, and have not sought the LORD: therefore they shall not prosper, and all their flocks shall be scattered.*

"FOR THE PASTORS ARE BECOME BRUTISH AND HAVE NOT SOUGHT THE LORD!"

The word BRUTISH here in this context literally means stupid! "For the pastors are become STUPID, and have not sought the LORD!" What is wrong with our churches today?

Jeremiah 12:2 *Thou hast planted them, yea, they have taken root: they grow, yea, they bring forth fruit: thou art near in their mouth, and far from their reins.*

"THOU ART NEAR IN THEIR MOUTH, AND FAR FROM THEIR REINS"

What comes out of one's mouth is not always what is in their heart. Too often, the child of God talks of godly things, but their heart is not near to God at all. Man looks on the outward appearance, but God sees the heart. It is what is in the heart of man that ultimately drives him in the direction he will go. Let our mouths line up with our hearts.

135

Jeremiah 12:10 *Many pastors have destroyed my vineyard, they have trodden my portion under foot, they have made my pleasant portion a desolate wilderness.*

"MANY PASTORS HAVE DESTROYED MY VINEYARD"

The term "pastor" means shepherd, and in this text, a shepherd allows his sheep to break down the fence surrounding a vineyard and allows the sheep to destroy what has been taken care of for so long. Many a pastor has taken the reigns of a ministry and torn down the fences, so to speak, only to see that ministry destroyed. Likewise, the children of Israel had been given a land manicured by God's own hand, only to have its leadership allow the people to destroy it!

Jeremiah 15:16 *Thy words were found, and I did eat them; and thy word was unto me the joy and rejoicing of mine heart: for I am called by thy name, O LORD God of hosts.*

"AND THY WORD WAS UNTO ME THE JOY AND REJOICING OF MINE HEART"

To hear from God ought to bring joy and be a cause for rejoicing. To many, it is a chore and a burden. The child longs for the comfort of the parent; so should we long to hear words of comfort from our Father.

Jeremiah 17:12 *A glorious high throne from the beginning is the place of our sanctuary.*

"A GLORIOUS HIGH THRONE...IS THE PLACE OF OUR SANCTUARY"

Too often, we seek comfort from the physical things of this earth. We look for deliverance and seek safety in the political leadership of our nation. Our sanctuary sits on a high throne above and beyond anything or anyone upon this earth, and His name is KING OF KINGS AND LORD OF LORDS!

Jeremiah 20:9 *Then I said, I will not make mention of him, nor speak any more in his name. But his word was in mine heart as a burning fire shut up in my bones, and I was weary with forbearing, and I could not stay.*

"BUT HIS WORD WAS IN MINE HEART AS A BURNING FIRE SHUT UP IN MY BONES"

Though weary and at times wanting to quit, the prophet declares that he must not; but rather, there is a fire that is building inside him so fierce that it must be turned loose. He must vent, he must tell someone, he must not quit! Let that same fire burn within us! The Holy Spirit in us cannot be contained nor snuffed out. Hebrews 12:29 says, "For our God is a consuming fire." A Christian will not quit. For if the Holy Spirit truly inhabits our body as a temple, then it cannot do anything but reveal the glory of God!

Jeremiah 21:8 *And unto this people thou shalt say, Thus saith the LORD; Behold, I set before you the way of life, and the way of death.*

"I SET BEFORE YOU THE WAY OF LIFE, AND THE WAY OF DEATH"

God has set before us two paths. Broad is the way that leadeth to destruction, but straight is the gate that leadeth to life. Yet, everyone will choose a path, and everyone will pick a destination. You will either choose destruction or restoration!
In every action we take, there is always a choice. It has been said that there are two sides to every door and two sides to every coin, and there are two sides to every story. Thus in life, there are two choices in regard to the paths that we take. One is a path of life; the other is a path of death. Which path have you chosen?

Jeremiah 21:14 *But I will punish you according to the fruit of your doings, saith the LORD: and I will kindle a fire in the forest thereof, and it shall devour all things round about it.*

"BUT I WILL PUNISH YOU ACCORDING TO THE FRUIT OF YOUR DOINGS"

For you shall be known by your fruit, whether good or bad. By that fruit, you shall reap either blessing or cursing!

Jeremiah 22:13 *Woe unto him that buildeth his house by unrighteousness, and his chambers by wrong; that useth his neighbour's service without wages, and giveth him not for his work;*

"WOE UNTO HIM THAT BUILDETH HIS HOUSE BY UNRIGHTEOUSNESS"

Honesty is a rare trait, sadly even among Christians! In all of our doings, let us be upright and live lives of integrity and honesty!

Jeremiah 28:13 *Go and tell Hananiah, saying, Thus saith the LORD; Thou hast broken the yokes of wood; but thou shalt make for them yokes of iron.*

"THOU HAST BROKEN THE YOKES OF WOOD"

God had commanded Jeremiah to prophecy with a yoke of wood around his neck, symbolizing the bondage Israel would be under at the hand of the Babylonian Empire and Nebuchadnezzar. A false prophet named Hananiah stepped up and proclaimed that all would be back to normal within two years. In making this statement, Hananiah took the wood yoke off of Jeremiah and broke it; however, God had said that the bondage would last seventy years. Man's words are like wood, hay, and stubble, easily broken. God's words are as iron—unmovable, unshakable, and unable to be broken.

Jeremiah 31:2 *Thus saith the LORD, The people which were left of the sword found grace in the wilderness; even Israel, when I went to cause him to rest.*

"FOUND GRACE IN THE WILDERNESS"

The children of Israel, though in captivity, were given a promise that they would not be left in bondage. How good it is to know that God never forsakes His own. Though we may be going through a valley in our life, we can still find grace in the wilderness. We can find peace in the promise that God will bring the trial to an end.

Jeremiah 31:17 *And there is hope in thine end, saith the LORD, that thy children shall come again to their own border.*

"AND THERE IS HOPE IN THINE END"

What a wonderful message to a nation in bondage. There is hope! Likewise, that same message still rings true today, for this is not the end. No matter the struggle or the trial, we can say with confidence that we have hope, for that very hope is in Jesus Christ and the sure return for His people.

Jeremiah 31:25 *For I have satiated the weary soul, and I have replenished every sorrowful soul.*

"FOR I HAVE SATIATED THE WEARY SOUL"

Oh soul, are you weary and troubled? Are you discouraged? God has satisfied the weary and replenished the sorrowful! Rise up and be of good cheer!

Jeremiah 31:33 *But this shall be the covenant, that I will make with the house of Israel; After those days, saith the Lord, I will put my law in their inward parts, and write it in their hearts; and will be their God, and they shall be my people.*

"I WILL PUT MY LAW IN THEIR INWARD PARTS...AND THEY SHALL BE MY PEOPLE"

"Thy Word have I hid in mine heart, that I might not sin against thee." A child of God will apply the Word of God to his heart. It becomes who we are. One cannot declare himself a child of God and not desire His Word.

Jeremiah 32:17 *Ah Lord GOD! behold, thou hast made the heaven and the earth by thy great power and stretched out arm, and there is nothing too hard for thee:*

"AND THERE IS NOTHING TO HARD FOR THEE"

A truth that needs to be understood by all Christians! There is nothing that God cannot handle or accomplish. Just because He can does not mean He will. Let us face each challenge with an understanding that we belong to a God who can move mountains if He so chooses!

Jeremiah 32:27 *Behold, I am the LORD, the God of all flesh: is there any thing too hard for me?*

"IS THERE ANY THING TOO HARD FOR ME"

A question deserves an answer! God asks if there is there anything too hard that He cannot handle? There is nothing he cannot accomplish. But another questions we may ask is "Is there anything too hard?" Is there anything that God might strain at doing? The answer is...NOTHING! There is nothing in our lives that our God cannot handle!

Jeremiah 38:20 *But Jeremiah said, They shall not deliver thee. Obey, I beseech thee, the voice of the LORD, which I speak unto thee: so it shall be well unto thee, and thy soul shall live.*

"OBEY, I BESEECH THEE, THE VOICE OF THE LORD"

The average church attendee fails to apply the message heard to their hearts and lives. The prophet Jeremiah cried out, "OBEY, I beseech thee." He begged them to listen to the voice of the Lord. When the Word of God is preached, we need to do more than just listen; we must apply what we have heard as well.

Jeremiah 42:3 *That the LORD thy God may shew us the way wherein we may walk, and the thing that we may do.*

"THAT THE LORD THY GOD MAY SHEW US THE WAY..."

Oh Lord, show us the way wherein we may walk and the thing that we may do! Let us always seek His face in every decision we make!

Jeremiah 42:20 *For ye dissembled in your hearts, when ye sent me unto the LORD your God, saying, Pray for us unto the LORD our God; and according unto all that the LORD our God shall say, so declare unto us, and we will do it.*

"FOR YE DISSEMBLED IN YOUR HEARTS"

A dissemblance of one's heart is to hide under false pretenses or to disguise one's true identity through false appearance or speech. The children of Israel came to Jeremiah asking for prayer in regard to God's direction but then refused to accept the answer. We often pray for God's will, but our hearts must be ready to accept God's will.

Jeremiah 42:22 *Now therefore know certainly that ye shall die by the sword, by the famine, and by the pestilence, in the place whither ye desire to go and to sojourn.*

"NOW THEREFORE KNOW CERTAINLY THAT YE SHALL DIE BY THE SWORD"

The warning had been given was yet not heeded. Israel would not change her ways and seek God's face, but rather she choose her own self-indulgence. Thus, the land of Judah was given over to destruction and death by the sword. There is still a call for repentance even today, and yet the same response is heard. What will it take for this nation to change her ways? Perhaps she must fall to the sword!

Jeremiah 49:7 *Concerning Edom, thus saith the LORD of hosts; Is wisdom no more in Teman? is counsel perished from the prudent? is their wisdom vanished?*

"IS COUNSEL PERISHED FROM THE PRUDENT"

Just before the destruction of any nation, there seems to be a lack of wisdom and counsel, such as it was with Edom. A lesson to be learned: let us seek good counsel and wisdom, lest we find ourselves destroyed!

Jeremiah 50:6 *My people hath been lost sheep: their shepherds have caused them to go astray, they have turned them away on the mountains: they have gone from mountain to hill, they have forgotten their restingplace.*

"THEY HAVE GONE FROM MOUNTAIN TO HILL"

The children looked to other gods for salvation. The appearance of others' success can be deceiving and draw us away to the extent that we begin to act and partake in their ways. Nothing and no nation can withstand God's power so much that He cannot have them removed and destroyed. The child of God who steps out from underneath the hand and direction of God to trust earthly strength and powers is giving up the refuge of a mountaintop for a hill.

GLEANINGS FROM THE BOOK OF LAMENTATIONS

Lamentations 1:1 *How doth the city sit solitary, that was full of people! how is she become as a widow! she that was great among the nations, and princess among the provinces, how is she become tributary!*

"HOW DOTH THE CITY SIT SOLITARY"

This is a statement and not a question. The warnings have been given and ignored. Nothing remains to be said but to grieve over the end result. Such is the working of sin. Sin, when it is finished, can destroy a life and ultimately the soul.

Lamentations 1:16 *For these things I weep; mine eye, mine eye runneth down with water, because the comforter that should relieve my soul is far from me: my children are desolate, because the enemy prevailed.*

"MY CHILDREN ARE DESOLATE, BECAUSE THE ENEMY PREVAILED"

There is nothing left of Judah to be passed on to the next generation because the enemy prevailed. The children must reap the sins of their fathers. Lord, help us, this generation who allow the enemy to prevail and refuse to acknowledge you as their Savior. The children are left desolate with no spiritual or Godly example to follow. Their heritage is destruction, ruin, and ungodliness. It is our job to train a child in the way that they should go, and yet we allow the enemy to prevail!

Lamentations 3:22 *It is of the LORD'S mercies that we are not consumed, because his compassions fail not.* **23** *They are new every morning: great is thy faithfulness.*

"GREAT IS THY FAITHFULNESS"

How interesting these verses are, considering the context in which they dwell: the lamenting of the destruction of Jerusalem! Even in the midst of the darkest trial, GOD IS FAITHFUL! For we are not consumed, His compassion never fails, and His mercies are new with every rising of the sun!

GLEANINGS FROM THE BOOK OF EZEKIEL

Ezekiel 3:10 *Moreover he said unto me, Son of man, all my words that I shall speak unto thee receive in thine heart, and hear with thine ears.*

"RECEIVE IN THINE HEART, AND HEAR WITH THINE EARS"

We are to receive what God says with an open heart and then hear from God. Hearing without having an open heart is futile. "Thy Word have I hid in mine heart, that I might not sin against thee."

Ezekiel 3:20 *Again, When a righteous man doth turn from his righteousness, and commit iniquity, and I lay a stumbling block before him, he shall die: because thou hast not given him warning, he shall die in his sin, and his righteousness which he hath done shall not be remembered; but his blood will I require at thine hand.*

"BUT HIS BLOOD WILL I REQUIRE AT THINE HAND"

God gives a stern warning to Ezekiel. God had given him a message to preach. If he fails then all who die because Ezekiel failed to relay the message, their blood would be on his hands. Those who die and go to Hell when we could have shared the salvation message with them, do we not likewise bear the responsibility of their souls?

Ezekiel 10:18 *Then the glory of the LORD departed from off the threshold of the house, and stood over the cherubims.*

"THEN THE GLORY OF THE LORD DEPARTED"

The children of Israel associated God's presence with the physical building of the temple. In the previous chapters, God rebukes them for their sinful actions. Ezekiel is then shown how God's temple was being used for false worship. The glory of God departs from the temple. Oh, that the glory of God would fall on our churches and not depart.

Ezekiel 12:2 *Son of man, thou dwellest in the midst of a rebellious house, which have eyes to see, and see not; they have ears to hear, and hear not: for they are a rebellious house.*

"FOR THEY ARE A REBELLIOUS HOUSE"

The definition of rebellion is clearly laid out by God: When the truth is in front of you but you refuse to see. When what is truth is told to you, but you refuse to hear. Not that you can't see or can't hear but choose to do it your way instead of God's way therefore anything contrary to Scripture is rebellion.

Ezekiel 16:15 *But thou didst trust in thine own beauty, and playedst the harlot because of thy renown, and pouredst out thy fornications on every one that passed by; his it was.*

"BUT THOU DIDST TRUST IN THINE OWN BEAUTY"

As we get older, we lose our youthfulness. We slow down and groan with aches and pains. Wrinkles and ailments set in, and yet we think we can trust in our own beauty. Sinful lusts of our youth are but for a season; then we must deal with eternity. His beauty is that of the rose of Sharon. When our looks fail and fade away, our beauty can be found in the beauty of Christ!

Ezekiel 18:31 *Cast away from you all your transgressions, whereby ye have transgressed; and make you a new heart and a new spirit: for why will ye die, O house of Israel?*

"FOR WHY WILL YE DIE"

Why would someone choose death over life? Are life's pleasures worth such a choice? Sin only brings joy for a season, but Christ gives an everlasting joy that cannot be taken away. Why then would someone make such a choice?

Ezekiel 22:30 *And I sought for a man among them, that should make up the hedge, and stand in the gap before me for the land, that I should not destroy it: but I found none.*

"BUT I FOUND NONE"

God is always searching for a man to stand out from the crowd, one worthy to stand before God on behalf of the people. Israel had leadership, but they were as corrupt as the nation itself. I wonder if God looked on America today if he would say the same thing...
BUT I FOUND NONE!

Ezekiel 23:39 *For when they had slain their children to their idols, then they came the same day into my sanctuary to profane it; and, lo, thus have they done in the midst of mine house.*

"THEN THEY CAME THE SAME DAY"

The people were offering their children up to idols and committing the most vile of sin in the name of other gods and then on the same day entering into the temple to worship the God of Heaven. This type of life is called an abomination. God would rather you be hot or cold, but a lukewarm Christian, He will spew out of His mouth.

Ezekiel 28:2 *Son of man, say unto the prince of Tyrus, Thus saith the Lord GOD; Because thine heart is lifted up, and thou hast said, I am a God, I sit in the seat of God, in the midst of the seas; yet thou art a man, and not God, though thou set thine heart as the heart of God:*

"BECAUSE THINE HEART IS LIFTED UP"

Pride is the doorway to destruction. God destroyed the enemies of Israel due to their pride. "Thou shalt have no other gods before me." Egyptian pharaohs thought themselves to be gods. God humbled Israel, but He promised destruction of Egypt. Pride is simply when one thinks he is god-like in his heart. Be careful that we don't elevate ourselves to thinking we are greater than we are.

Ezekiel 33:33 *And when this cometh to pass, (lo, it will come,) then shall they know that a prophet hath been among them.*

"THEN SHALL THEY KNOW THAT A PROPHET HATH BEEN AMONG THEM"

There will come a day when the lost will look back and say that those who believed and preached Jesus Christ were right. On that day, it will be too late. Ezekiel is called by God to be a watchman over the house of Israel, to give a warning. Though they may not heed the warning, that which the Lord hath said will come to pass and the people will one day realize that a prophet has been walking among them. We are even today called to be a witness to a darkened world, to plant that seed of hope. They may not initially listen; but one day, they may look back and say, "that Christian was right!"

Ezekiel 36:36 *Then the heathen that are left round about you shall know that I the LORD build the ruined places, and plant that that was desolate: I the LORD have spoken it, and I will do it.*

"...I THE LORD BUILD THE RUINED PLACES"

Not broken places but ruined places. Something broken can be repaired or fixed by man; but something ruined, only God can fix.

Ezekiel 46:9 *But when the people of the land shall come before the LORD in the solemn feasts, he that entereth in by the way of the north gate to worship shall go out by the way of the south gate; and he that entereth by the way of the south gate shall go forth by the way of the north gate: he shall not return by the way of the gate whereby he came in, but shall go forth over against it.*

"HE SHALL NOT RETURN BY THE WAY OF THE GATE WHEREBY HE CAME IN"

Ezekiel is given insight to future events, a time when the temple will be rebuilt and the Lord's glory will return to the temple. All mankind will be able to enter in and see and experience that glory; however, they may enter one way but must leave another. Once someone has experienced the glory of God, you won't leave the same person you were before you met Christ.

GLEANINGS FROM THE BOOK OF DANIEL

Daniel 1:8 *But Daniel purposed in his heart that he would not defile himself with the portion of the king's meat, nor with the wine which he drank: therefore he requested of the prince of the eunuchs that he might not defile himself.*

"THAT HE MIGHT NOT DEFILE HIMSELF"

Eating meat would not defile Daniel; but rather, disobeying God's commands and being a part of the kings prideful plan to elevate himself by using Daniel would. Defile means to contaminate or to make impure. We as Christians must be careful in all that we do that we do not defile ourselves.

Daniel 2:22 *He revealeth the deep and secret things: he knoweth what is in the darkness, and the light dwelleth with him.*

"HE REVEALETH THE DEEP AND SECRET THINGS: HE KNOWETH WHAT IS IN THE DARKNESS"

That thing that you have hidden, that thought, that sin that no one knows, your deepest darkest secrets you have hidden in hopes that no one will know, are all revealed in the light of His glory! What may be hidden to man's eyes cannot be hidden from God.

Daniel 2:28 *But there is a God in heaven that revealeth secrets, and maketh known to the king Nebuchadnezzar what shall be in the latter days. Thy dream, and the visions of thy head upon thy bed, are these;*

"BUT THERE IS A GOD IN HEAVEN THAT REVEALETH SECRETS"

There is a God! Let the unbelieving scoff and curse, but there is a God, and Heaven is His throne room! The God of Heaven is a revealer of secrets! To be a revealer of secrets, one must know the heart! Yes, there is a God, and nothing is beyond His power or the reach of His hand!

Daniel 6:10 *Now when Daniel knew that the writing was signed, he went into his house; and his windows being open in his chamber toward Jerusalem, he kneeled upon his knees three times a day, and prayed, and gave thanks before his God, as he did aforetime.*

"AND GAVE THANKS BEFORE HIS GOD"

Daniel knows that he is headed for the lion's den, and yet there is no hesitation to continue to be thankful. No matter the circumstances, we should always be thankful. God was good before, He is good now, and He will be good tomorrow!

Daniel 6:26 *I make a decree, That in every dominion of my kingdom men tremble and fear before the God of Daniel: for he is the living God, and stedfast for ever, and his kingdom that which shall not be destroyed, and his dominion shall be even unto the end.*

"FOR HE IS THE LIVING GOD, AND STEADFAST FOR EVER"

Our God is a living God. It is not that He is alive but that our God cannot be killed! Nothing can harm the God of Heaven! He is steadfast, immovable, unshakeable forever! HALLELUJAH!

Daniel 12:2 *And many of them that sleep in the dust of the earth shall awake, some to everlasting life, and some to shame and everlasting contempt.*

"SOME TO EVERLASTING LIFE, AND SOME TO SHAME AND EVERLASTING CONTEMPT"

Yes, there is coming a day when all will meet God face to face! How you meet God is your choice. You can by faith accept Christ and have everlasting life or stand before God in shame and have everlasting contempt! The choice is yours!

GLEANINGS FROM THE BOOK OF HOSEA

Hosea 4:*1 Hear the word of the LORD, ye children of Israel: for the LORD hath a controversy with the inhabitants of the land, because there is no truth, nor mercy, nor knowledge of God in the land.*

"HEAR THE WORD OF THE LORD"

When we refuse to hear the word of the Lord, there is no truth, no mercy, and no knowledge of God! The foolish statements often spoken by both the lost and even at times the child of God prove that they have no knowledge of who God really is. We are called to study to show ourselves approved unto God, a workman that needeth not to be ashamed, but rightly dividing the word of truth. God is truth, and to know Him is to know truth.

Hosea 4:6 *My people are destroyed for lack of knowledge: because thou hast rejected knowledge, I will also reject thee, that thou shalt be no priest to me: seeing thou hast forgotten the law of thy God, I will also forget thy children.*

"MY PEOPLE ARE DESTROYED FOR LACK OF KNOWLEDGE"

We are told in scripture to study to show ourselves approved unto God. This is not just a spiritual concept but one to be applied in everyday life, for knowledge and understanding give us a plan of action! Without knowledge, how can we move forward? Thus, we simply sit and wait to be destroyed.

Hosea 6:1 *Come, and let us return unto the LORD: for he hath torn, and he will heal us; he hath smitten, and he will bind us* up.

"COME, AND LET US RETURN UNTO THE LORD"

How long will you run from the Lord? What will it take for you to return to the Lord? Will you fall under the chastisement of God? If we will but cease from wickedness and seek His face, He will heal and mend the broken of heart.

Hosea 11:6 *And the sword shall abide on his cities, and shall consume his branches, and devour them, because of their own counsels.*

"BECAUSE OF THEIR OWN COUNSELS"

Hosea is a call to faithfulness. Much of Israel's downfall can be summed up in this verse. They simply looked to their own counsel. They did that which they thought was right in their own eyes. Let the just live by faith and not by sight. We must trust in God for His direction.

Hosea 14:1 *O Israel, return unto the LORD thy God; for thou hast fallen by thine iniquity.* **2** *Take with you words, and turn to the LORD: say unto him, Take away all iniquity, and receive us graciously: so will we render the calves of our lips.*

"FOR THOU HAST FALLEN BY THINE INIQUITY"

A cry for the backslidden nation of Israel to confess and return unto the Lord. I can't help but think that this same call from God is applicable to His people today! Let us put away our sin and draw nigh unto Him!

GLEANINGS FROM THE BOOK OF JOEL

Joel 3:12 *Let the heathen be wakened, and come up to the valley of Jehoshaphat: for there will I sit to judge all the heathen round about.*

"LET THE HEATHEN BE WAKENED"

Heathen, by definition, means to be pagan. God is calling out the children of Israel to take up the sword and to stop acting like the pagan people that were out to destroy them. In short, Israel had become like their enemy when they should have been fighting their enemy. Likewise, we as Christians ought not act like the heathen world but rather put on the whole armor of God!

GLEANINGS FROM THE BOOK OF AMOS

Amos 4:12 *Therefore thus will I do unto thee, O Israel: and because I will do this unto thee, prepare to meet thy God, O Israel.*

"PREPARE TO MEET THY GOD"

As God declared to Israel, so it is no different with us! There is a day coming where we will all stand and give an account. What is your current state of being? Could it be that there are preparations to be addressed? PREPARE TO MEET THY GOD!

Amos 8:11 *Behold, the days come, saith the Lord GOD, that I will send a famine in the land, not a famine of bread, nor a thirst for water, but of hearing the words of the LORD:*

"BUT OF HEARING THE WORDS OF THE LORD"

Not unlike the days of Joel, so are we today in the midst of a famine: not a famine for lack of food but rather a spiritual famine. Our churches are empty, our Bibles are unopened and collecting dust, and our houses of worship are but empty, if not closed altogether. Amos had prophesied of a coming famine brought in by fire and grasshoppers, but the real famine was a spiritual one in the hearts of God's people. Today is no different. The church houses are empty on Sunday, Bibles are not read, and the prayer closet is not used. Lord, help us to hunger for Your Word.

GLEANINGS FROM THE BOOK OF JONAH

Jonah 1:5 *Then the mariners were afraid, and cried every man unto his god, and cast forth the wares that were in the ship into the sea, to lighten it of them. But Jonah was gone down into the sides of the ship; and he lay, and was fast asleep.*

"AND HE LAY, AND WAS FAST ASLEEP"

The storm was such that the mariners were throwing things overboard and crying out to their gods in fear, and yet Jonah was asleep in the hull of the ship. While the storms of life rage around us and humanity cries for help seeking their own gods, we as Christians are safe in the shelter of our ship of salvation. How often do we live asleep and rest in the safety of our Savior, and yet there is a world dying and on their way to a devil's Hell?

Jonah 1:6 *So the shipmaster came to him, and said unto him, What meanest thou, O sleeper? arise, call upon thy God, if so be that God will think upon us, that we perish not.*

"WHAT MEANEST THOU, O SLEEPER"

What purpose does a child of God have to sleep when so many are perishing? Arise out of your slumber, oh Christian, and cry out to God! Arise, oh Christian, and take action! Why would we sleep while others perish? Very interesting how a pagan ship captain questions Jonah's motives. Even the pagan are watching to see if our faith is real. It could be that unbelievers are the way they are because we are asleep!

Jonah 2:7 *When my soul fainted within me I remembered the LORD: and my prayer came in unto thee, into thine holy temple.*

"WHEN MY SOUL FAINTED WITHIN ME I REMEMBERED THE LORD"

There is no greater peace within the heart of a Christian than to know that when all others have failed you and when all effort has fallen short, when all seems to be lost, there is One who sits on the throne, and HIS NAME IS THE LORD! Take comfort this morning, dear Christian, for as Jonah said, "MY PRAYER CAME IN UNTO THEE." So shall our prayers reach the ear of the Father!

GLEANINGS FROM THE BOOK OF MICAH

Micah 6:2 *Hear ye, O mountains, the LORD'S controversy, and ye strong foundations of the earth: for the LORD hath a controversy with his people, and he will plead with Israel.*

"FOR THE LORD HATH A CONTROVERSY WITH HIS PEOPLE"

God pleads with Judah to seek the Lord rather than their greed and desire for personal gain. Micah responds with a question. He asks how many sacrifices can be made to gain God's mercy. How often do we try to out give God when, in reality, God does not need our money or belongings but rather our faithfulness?

Micah 6:8 *He hath shewed thee, O man, what is good; and what doth the LORD require of thee, but to do justly, and to love mercy, and to walk humbly with thy God?*

"WHAT DOTH THE LORD REQUIRE OF THEE"

It is our reasonable service to live a just life, one that is upright and free of evil actions, that shows kindness to all people, and to love and walk with God daily! What doth the Lord require of thee today?

Micah 7:7 *Therefore I will look unto you the Lord: I will wait for the God of my salvation: my God will hear me.*

"I WILL WAIT FOR THE GOD OF MY SALVATION"

The waiting is the hardest part. Timing is everything. Patience is a virtue. God hears the cry of the righteous, and He knows our every need. He will provide when we need it most.

GLEANINGS FROM THE BOOK OF NAHUM

Nahum 1:7 *The LORD is good, a strong hold in the day of trouble; and he knoweth them that trust in him.*

"A STRONG HOLD IN THE DAY OF TROUBLE"

The previous verses give us a description of God's power and authority. The God that spoke the world into existence is the God that can move mountains and dry up rivers simply at His presence. This same power becomes our stronghold in our time of need. Why should we feel discouraged when trials come when His very presence can shatter the darkest of times?

GLEANINGS FROM THE BOOK OF HABAKKUK

Habakkuk 2:4 *Behold, his soul which is lifted up is not upright in him: but the just shall live by his faith.*

"BUT THE JUST SHALL LIVE BY HIS FAITH"

A Christian lives by his faith. Not by someone else's, but by how strong your faith is. How we deal with the things of this world is based upon the strength of our faith!

Habakkuk 3:2 *O LORD, I have heard thy speech, and was afraid: O LORD, revive thy work in the midst of the years, in the midst of the years make known; in wrath remember mercy.*

"O LORD, REVIVE THY WORK IN THE MIDST OF THE YEARS!"

In the middle of an invasion by the Babylonian Empire. In the middle of unrest and pagan worship. In the middle of political unrest and division. In the middle of your life, yet it is not to late or too far gone for God to revive a work!
I fear that the days of revival are gone! Lord how we need it!
Revive us again!
Fill each heart with Thy love!
May each soul be rekindled
With fire from above!

GLEANINGS FROM THE BOOK OF HAGGAI

Haggai 1:7 *Now therefore thus saith the LORD of hosts; Consider your ways.*

"THUS SAITH THE LORD OF HOSTS; CONSIDER YOUR WAYS"

It would do many a man well to consider his ways! This includes both the manner in which we live as well as the direction we choose to take our lives. The Lord would have us consider our ways. Is the way we are choosing of God?

Haggai 1:14 *And the LORD stirred up the spirit of Zerubbabel the son of Shealtiel, governor of Judah, and the spirit of Joshua the son of Josedech, the high priest, and the spirit of all the remnant of the people; and they came and did work in the house of the LORD of hosts, their God,*

"AND THEY CAME AND DID WORK IN THE HOUSE OF THE LORD OF HOST, THEIR GOD"

The Holy Spirit compelled men to do a work in the Lord's house. Not just any house, but of the One they call God! If the work of the church is to be accomplished, it must include God the Father, God the Son, and God the Holy Spirit!

GLEANINGS FROM THE BOOK OF ZECHARIAH

Zechariah 7:9 *Thus speaketh the LORD of hosts, saying, Execute true judgment, and shew mercy and compassions every man to his brother:* **10** *And oppress not the widow, nor the fatherless, the stranger, nor the poor; and let none of you imagine evil against his brother in your heart.*

"EXECUTE TRUE JUDGEMENT"

The question of whether they should continue fasting in the fifth month as they had done for the past seventy years. Yet, God responds with something far better than ritualistic tradition. True judgment is far better than ceremony.

Zechariah 13:1 *In that day there shall be a fountain opened to the house of David and to the inhabitants of Jerusalem for sin and for uncleanness.*

"IN THAT DAY THERE SHALL BE A FOUNTAIN"

The prophecy of Zechariah of a coming Savior who would wash away their sins. He did come, and His name was Jesus! "There is a fountain filled with blood drawn from Immanuel's veins, and sinners plunged beneath that flood lose all their guilty stains."

GLEANINGS FROM THE BOOK OF MALACHI

Malachi 3:8 *Will a man rob God? Yet ye have robbed me. But ye say, Wherein have we robbed thee? In tithes and offerings.*

"IN TITHES AND OFFERINGS"

In Malachi 1:14, God called the children of Israel deceivers in regard to their offerings. They were giving, but what they were giving and how they were giving it was the problem. Oftentimes, we make ourselves feel good by putting something in the offering plate when, in reality, it's not about feeling good at all. One who gives out of love will give all that they have.

Malachi 4:2 *But unto you that fear my name shall the Sun of righteousness arise with healing in his wings; and ye shall go forth, and grow up as calves of the stall.*

"BUT UNTO YOU THAT FEAR MY NAME SHALL THE SUN OF RIGHTEOUSNESS ARISE WITH HEALING IN HIS WINGS"

Good to know that in our time of need "THE SUN OF RIGHTEOUSNESS (shall) ARISE WITH HEALING IN HIS WINGS."

GLEANINGS FROM THE BOOK OF MATTHEW

Matthew 3:1 *In those days came John the Baptist, preaching in the wilderness of Judaea,*

"PREACHING IN THE WILDERNESS OF JUDAEA"

The Jews say that much has come out of the wilderness. It was in the wilderness that God gave the Ten Commandments. It was in the wilderness that the tabernacle was established. It was in the wilderness that the priesthood was put into place. Now we see a salvation message of repentance preached in the wilderness! It is in those times of wilderness wanderings that we need to be reminded of God's law, God's house, God's leadership, and God's message.

Matthew 3:15 *And Jesus answering said unto him, Suffer it to be so now: for thus it becometh us to fulfil all righteousness. Then he suffered him.*

"FOR THUS IT BECOMETH US TO FULFILL ALL RIGHTEOUSNESS"

How wonderful it is to be included in God's plan for the salvation of mankind. Jesus looked at John the Baptist and said, "It becometh us to fulfill righteousness." What an honor it is for Jesus to use me to fulfill His righteousness!

Matthew 4:17 *From that time Jesus began to preach, and to say, Repent: for the kingdom of heaven is at hand.*

"REPENT: FOR THE KINGDOM OF HEAVEN IS AT HAND"

The word "Christian" means to be Christlike. If we are to be as Christ, then we are to mimic His actions! Christ declared that the kingdom of Heaven was at hand and that all should repent! If there ever was a time to declare that all should repent, it is now! For the kingdom of Heaven is closer than ever before!

Matthew 5:45 *That ye may be the children of your Father which is in heaven: for he maketh his sun to rise on the evil and on the good, and sendeth rain on the just and on the unjust.*

"FOR HE MAKETH HIS SUN TO RISE ON THE EVIL AND ON THE GOOD"

The answer to the age-old question, "Why do bad things happen to good people?" Today, tragedy will make its way into the evil as well as the good. The saved and the unsaved both awake to the same sun. The difference is that we have a Comforter to help us through those times.

Matthew 6:30 *Wherefore, if God so clothe the grass of the field, which to day is, and to morrow is cast into the oven, shall he not much more clothe you, O ye of little faith?*

"O YE OF LITTLE FAITH"

The same God who provides the sunshine for the grass to grow is the same God that can provide for your every need! Have a little faith!

Matthew 7:5 *Thou hypocrite, first cast out the beam out of thine own eye; and then shalt thou see clearly to cast out the mote out of thy brother's eye.*

"AND THEN SHALT THOU SEE CLEARLY"

The criticism of Christians from one to another is addressed by our Savior. How quickly we point out the faults of others. An individual who is quick to criticize is, more often than not, dealing with their own issues. We must first clean up our own act; not so we have the liberty to criticize others but so that we can clearly see how to help our brothers and sisters in Christ.

Matthew 8:26 *And he saith unto them, Why are ye fearful, O ye of little faith? Then he arose, and rebuked the winds and the sea; and there was a great calm.*

"AND THERE WAS A GREAT CALM"

How interesting this passage is. A rebuke of His disciples, and then He rebuked the storm. When the words of Jesus are spoken, there is A GREAT CALM! A peace that passes all understanding. When this life's turbulent waves crash all around, let us retreat to His Word, for it is there we may find A GREAT CALM!

Matthew 11:9 *But what went ye out for to see? A prophet? yea, I say unto you, and more than a prophet.*

"BUT WHAT WENT YE OUT TO SEE"

A great question coming from our Savior. Jesus asked His disciples in regard to John the Baptist, "What went ye out to see?" Was it the way he was dressed in camel's hair? Was it to watch him eat locusts? Was it to see some spectacle, or did you go out to hear a prophet? Why do we go to church? Why do we pray and read our Bible? Is to see some miracle or spectacle? John the Baptist prepared the way of Jesus's coming. Could it be that we need to come seeking Jesus and not a spectacle?

Matthew 11:19 *The Son of man came eating and drinking, and they say, Behold a man gluttonous, and a winebibber, a friend of publicans and sinners. But wisdom is justified of her children.*

"BUT WISDOM IS JUSTIFIED OF HER CHILDREN"

John the Baptist, who was odd in his ways, was accused of being demon-possessed. Jesus, who associated himself with sinners, was accused of partaking in the same sins, such as gluttony and drunkenness. Jesus responded by saying that "wisdom is justified of her children." The truth would be revealed in those that accepted and believed truth. The wisdom of Christ would change the hearts of men while His accusers remain in their sin.

Matthew 12:34 *O generation of vipers, how can ye, being evil, speak good things? for out of the abundance of the heart the mouth speaketh.*

"FOR OUT OF THE ABUNDANCE OF THE HEART THE MOUTH SPEAKETH"

How can someone who is evil speak good things? How can someone heed the counsel of one who is evil in his actions? Saying and doing are two completely different things. If evil is what a man lives and consumes, then evil is what will come out of his mouth!

Mathew 13:58 *And he did not many mighty works there because of their unbelief.*

"BECAUSE OF THEIR UNBELIEF"

How many times do we miss the great and wondrous works of our Lord due to our unbelief? He did not mighty works because of unbelief. How quickly we forget that the faith of a mustard seed moves mountains!

Matthew 16:12 *Then understood they how that he bade them not beware of the leaven of bread, but of the doctrine of the Pharisees and of the Sadducees.*

"BEWARE...BUT OF THE DOCTRINE OF THE PHARISEES AND OF THE SADDUCEES"

We should always seek out sound doctrine. However, Jesus warned us against the doctrine of the Pharisees and of the Sadducees. One of hypocrisy and the other of worldliness and self indulgence! Of such people, we should show great caution in regard to sound doctrine!

Matthew 17:24 *And when they were come to Capernaum, they that received tribute money came to Peter, and said, Doth not your master pay tribute?*

"DOTH NOT YOUR MASTER PAY TRIBUTE"

It is somewhat comical to hear someone ask if Jesus gives to His own house. For indeed He did, but not the half shekel that was required. Rather, he gave His life. Even the Master, so as not to offend (though He did not have to), gave an offering. Something to think about this morning.

Matthew 20:33 *They say unto him, Lord, that our eyes may be opened.*

"THAT OUR EYES MAY BE OPENED"

Certainly these two blind men wanted their physical blindness healed, and with that healing came a spiritual awakening as well! OH THAT OUR EYES WOULD BE OPENED SPIRITUALLY!

Matthew 22:29 *Jesus answered and said unto them, Ye do err, not knowing the scriptures, nor the power of God.*

"YE DO ERR"

The question is in regard to a woman being married multiple times on earth: whose wife she will be in Heaven? Jesus's response was pointed, for He replied, "Ye do err." How did they err? The same way even today men do err! How? Not knowing the Scriptures and not knowing the power of God!

Matthew 23:11 *But he that is greatest among you shall be your servant.*

"BUT HE THAT IS GREATEST"

A recipe for greatness! In the eyes of God, the matter of who is great does not depend on one's talent or athletic ability but on a servant's heart! The one who serves the Lord is considered great in the eyes of God!

Matthew 24:44 *Therefore be ye also ready: for in such an hour as ye think not the Son of man cometh.*

"THEREFORE BE YE ALSO READY"

Because we know not the exact moment, let us then be ready! For when you are not expecting His return, like a thief in the night He will appear! Are you ready to meet Him?

Matthew 26:15 *And said unto them, What will ye give me, and I will deliver him unto you? And they covenanted with him for thirty pieces of silver.*

"WHAT WILL YE GIVE ME"

In today's currency, thirty pieces of silver is worth, give or take, two hundred dollars. Judas asked this question: "What will ye give me to betray Him?" What is His betrayal worth to you? A day at the beach? The grass mowed? A football game? Perhaps just a nap or longer time in bed. What is keeping us from prayer, time in His Word, or starting our week in His house? What will you accept to betray the Lord?

Thirty pieces of silver was not a great deal of money. In fact, Exodus 21:32 states that it is the same price for a slave to pull a cart in the place of an ox. Not a servant, but a slave to be whipped and driven like an animal. We have a choice to willingly serve the master or sell ourselves to be a slave to sin. The servant gains rewards for his service, while the slave is left to die when he is no longer needed. Man cannot serve two masters. We must all choose!

GLEANINGS FROM THE BOOK OF MARK

Mark 3:8 *And from Jerusalem, and from Idumaea, and from beyond Jordan; and they about Tyre and Sidon, a great multitude, when they had heard what great things he did, came unto him.*

"WHEN THEY HEARD WHAT GREAT THINGS HE DID"

Earlier, Jesus had healed a leper. Though he commanded that the leper tell no one, the excitement and joy could not be contained. When they heard of the healing and goodness of Jesus, they came from all over. Let us likewise tell everyone we meet of the good things that God has done for us.

Mark 4:38 *And he was in the hinder part of the ship, asleep on a pillow: and they awake him, and say unto him, Master, carest thou not that we perish? 39 And he arose, and rebuked the wind, and said unto the sea, Peace, be still. And the wind ceased, and there was a great calm.*

"CAREST THOU NOT THAT WE PERISH"

How many times have we lifted our eyes and cried out this very same thing? How often we forget that he still has the power to speak "PEACE BE STILL!" If we will take a moment and listen this morning, it could be that we will find "A GREAT CALM!"

Mark 4:40 *And he said unto them, Why are ye so fearful? how is it that ye have no faith?*

"HOW IS IT THAT YE HAVE NO FAITH"

How is it that a Christian has no faith? The disciples were amazed at Jesus's rebuke of the storm. They had seen Jesus heal the sick, but to rebuke the elements was something completely different! A Christian's faith will grow with each new encounter with Jesus. Christians today lack in faith due to not seeing and experiencing what God can do in their lives! Faith cometh by hearing and hearing through the Word of God. Show me a Christian who fails to pray, read their Bible, and sit under sound preaching, and I will show you a Christian who lacks faith!

Mark 5:35 *While he yet spake, there came from the ruler of the synagogue's house certain which said, Thy daughter is dead: why troublest thou the Master any further?*

"WHY TROUBLEST THOU THE MASTER ANY FURTHER"

Jairus, a ruler of the synagogue, desired that Jesus come and heal his daughter. Jairus had position, wealth, and popularity, but none of that could heal the daughter he loved so dearly. A servant arrived and declared that it was too late, for she was dead. There was no need to trouble the Master any further. Why troublest thou the Master any further? Because only the Master can address our deepest cares when all hope is gone!

Mark 7:6 *He answered and said unto them, Well hath Esaias prophesied of you hypocrites, as it is written, This people honoureth me with their lips, but their heart is far from me.*
21 *For from within, out of the heart of men, proceed evil thoughts, adulteries, fornications, murders,* **22** *Thefts, covetousness, wickedness, deceit, lasciviousness, an evil eye, blasphemy, pride, foolishness:* **23** *All these evil things come from within, and defile the man.*

"THIS PEOPLE HONOURETH ME WITH THEIR LIPS, BUT THEIR HEART IS FAR FROM ME"

A true definition of hypocrisy. The person who honors God with his mouth but whose heart is vile with sin. Lip service without the heart is nothing but noise. Man looks on the outward appearance but God sees the heart.

Mark 8:14 *Now the disciples had forgotten to take bread, neither had they in the ship with them more than one loaf.*

"NOW THE DISCIPLES HAD FORGOTTEN TO TAKE BREAD"

The account of the feeding of the four thousand. Jesus had compassion on the multitude and sought to feed them, both physically and spiritually. There were seven baskets left over, and yet the disciples straightway left the bread behind. Jesus, in verse seventeen, gets to the root of the problem when He asks, "Have ye your heart yet hardened?" The opposite of compassion is a hardened heart. How can we be in such a hurry as to not share Christ with others? It can be only the condition of our hearts.

Mark 9:24 *And straightway the father of the child cried out, and said with tears, Lord, I believe; help thou mine unbelief.*

"LORD, I BELIEVE; HELP THOU MINE UNBELIEF"

When the weight of the trial causes much doubt, we believe that God is real and true, and yet our discouragements cause us to doubt God's plan. Lord, give us strength to endure when we lack the vision to see clearly!

Mark 10:49 *And Jesus stood still, and commanded him to be called. And they call the blind man, saying unto him, Be of good comfort, rise; he calleth thee.*

"AND JESUS STOOD STILL"

What is it that makes Jesus stand still? What is it that causes the Master to stop and take notice? When a lost sinner cries out, "Have mercy on me."

Mark 11:25 *And when ye stand praying, forgive, if ye have ought against any: that your Father also which is in heaven may forgive you your trespasses.*

"AND WHEN YE STAND PRAYING, FORGIVE"

A key component in prayer is taught by our Lord. Prayer is a condition of the heart, for how can we kneel before the King of Kings and Lord of Lords with bitterness in our hearts? When we pray, we must come with a forgiving spirit. Do unto others as you would have done unto you. We must forgive if we expect to be forgiven.

Mark 12:27 *He is not the God of the dead, but the God of the living: ye therefore do greatly err.*

"HE IS NOT THE GOD OF THE DEAD"

Many a man will seek his god in a graveyard! If you seek your god at the foot of a tomb, then your god is dead! Our God is the God of the living. For in the person of Jesus Christ, He conquered death! Remember what the angel said at the tomb? "Why seek ye the living among the dead?" He is alive today and He is KING OF KINGS AND LORD OF LORDS!

GLEANINGS FROM THE BOOK OF LUKE

Luke 2:29 *Lord, now lettest thou thy servant depart in peace, according to thy word:* **30** *For mine eyes have seen thy salvation,*

"FOR MINE EYES HAVE SEEN THY SALVATION"

The account of Simeon and his declaration! He had waited his whole life to see the salvation of the Lord. Once he set his eyes on Jesus, he knew he could then die in peace. In the words of that old hymn, "Turn your eyes upon Jesus, look full in His wonderful face, and the things of Earth will grow strangely dim, in the light of His glory and grace." To face death without Christ is truly a fearful thing!

Luke 4:29 *And rose up, and thrust him out of the city, and led him unto the brow of the hill whereon their city was built, that they might cast him down headlong.*

"AND ROSE UP, AND THRUST HIM OUT OF THE CITY"

Jesus opens the scroll in the temple, reads the prophecy of Isaiah, and declares that He is the fulfillment of that prophecy. He is first thrust out of the temple, then out of the city, and finally, though unsuccessful, they attempted to kill Jesus altogether. When truth is revealed, it is sometimes hard to hear, and yet, instead of adhering to truth, we thrust it out.

Luke 6:35 *But love ye your enemies, and do good, and lend, hoping for nothing again; and your reward shall be great, and ye shall be the children of the Highest: for he is kind unto the unthankful and to the evil.*

"FOR HE IS KIND UNTO THE UNTHANKFUL AND TO THE EVIL"

A promise that kindness to those who despise us will reap great reward! For God Himself shows kindness to the undeserving and shows mercy to the most evil!

Luke 7:35 *But wisdom is justified of all her children.*

"BUT WISDOM IS JUSTIFIED"

There is an old saying that simply states, "The proof is in the pudding" or, simply stated, the end result speaks for itself! How quickly we judge others when, in reality, it is nothing more than jealousy. Wisdom is often criticized by the onlooker. Wisdom or no, the end result will speak for itself!

Luke 8:25 *And he said unto them, Where is your faith? And they being afraid wondered, saying one to another, What manner of man is this! for he commandeth even the winds and water, and they obey him.*

"AND HE SAID UNTO THEM, WHERE IS YOUR FAITH"

Nothing is truly lost, but rather misplaced. Perhaps even forgotten. Jesus asked His disciples a very pointed question. "Where is your faith?" Not that they did not have faith, but where was it? Their faith was in their own ability to get through the storm. We all have faith, but where and what we put our faith in is the ultimate question.

Luke 9:55 *But he turned, and rebuked them, and said, Ye know not what manner of spirit ye are of.*

"YE KNOW NOT WHAT MANNER OF SPIRIT YE ARE OF"

Jesus and His disciples had entered a village of the Samaritans, but the village did not give them a warm welcome. As they were leaving, James and John suggested that fire be called down from Heaven and consume the village. Jesus rebuked them! Our actions show forth the true spirit of whom we serve! Sad to say, there are many people who claim to be saved, but their actions seem to be of a different spirit!

Luke 12:6 *Are not five sparrows sold for two farthings, and not one of them is forgotten before God? 7 But even the very hairs of your head are all numbered. Fear not therefore: ye are of more value than many sparrows.*

"YE ARE OF MORE VALUE THAN MANY SPARROWS"

Not one of God's creations has been forgotten or is of no value to Him! Yet of all of God's creation, only man was given a soul. The God Who cares so deeply for the sparrow cares so much more for us, even to the very strand of hair on our heads. How much more then ought we to lay our cares at His feet!

Luke 12:51 *Suppose ye that I am come to give peace on earth? I tell you, Nay; but rather division:*

"NAY; BUT RATHER DIVISION"

That Jesus would state that He came to cause division on the surface might be a controversial statement. However, it is surely truth, for one must choose! Either God or the devil! Good or evil! Heaven or Hell! Friend, you are either saved or lost! Yes, Jesus surely came to cause a division! Which will you choose?

Luke 14:1 *And it came to pass, as he went into the house of one of the chief Pharisees to eat bread on the sabbath day, that they watched him.*

"THAT THEY WATCHED HIM"

Not all of the multitude that followed Christ followed Him with good intentions, but rather some observed with the intent to contradict Christ at every turn. The idea of being Christlike will result in many watching and observing with but one intent: to catch you in a fault. We must as Christians use caution; we are being watched for the intent of destroying our reputation and testimony.

Luke 16:15 *And he said unto them, Ye are they which justify yourselves before men; but God knoweth your hearts: for that which is highly esteemed among men is abomination in the sight of God.*

"YE ARE THEY WHICH JUSTIFY YOURSELVES BEFORE MEN; BUT GOD KNOWETH YOUR HEARTS"

The desire to have the recognition of man is considered an abomination to God! Not necessarily the act itself but the heart behind the action. To seek man's approval over God's is an issue of the heart. Let all that we do be done to glorify God and God alone.

Luke 17:5 *And the apostles said unto the Lord, Increase our faith.*

"INCREASE OUR FAITH"

In the very next chapter, in verse eight, Jesus Himself asked if when the Son of Man cometh, shall He find faith on the earth? Oh, that we as God's people would pray for an increase in our faith so that should Christ return at any moment, He should find us faithful!

Luke 17:29 *But the same day that Lot went out of Sodom it rained fire and brimstone from heaven, and destroyed them all.* **30** *Even thus shall it be in the day when the Son of man is revealed.*

"WHEN THE SON OF MAN IS REVEALED"

When the time of Christ's return arrives, there will be no time to make things right! In the days of Sodom, they ate and drank; then in a moment, they were consumed! Today is the day of salvation, for there may not be a tomorrow!

Luke 20:18 *Whosoever shall fall upon that stone shall be broken; but on whomsoever it shall fall, it will grind him to powder.*

"WHOSOEVER SHALL FALL UPON THAT STONE SHALL BE BROKEN"

Jesus is this cornerstone, but how interesting the context of this verse is. It is a verse of submission! You will either fall under this cornerstone and be crushed or fall on it and be changed! One submits to complete destruction while the other is simply broken. Broken means submissive to be used. For we can bow now, broken before Jesus, or bow later in destruction!

Luke 21:34 *And take heed to yourselves, lest at any time your hearts be overcharged with surfeiting, and drunkenness, and cares of this life, and so that day come upon you unawares.*

"AND SO THAT DAY COME UPON YOU UNAWARES"

The term "comfort food" might come into play here in this verse. When troublesome times come, often people turn to indulgences to numb the events of this life. Christ cautions His followers to not get caught up in the cares of this world nor its indulgences but rather to look to His coming insomuch that when He does come, we are prepared and not caught off guard.

Luke 22:40 *And when he was at the place, he said unto them, Pray that ye enter not into temptation.*
46 *And said unto them, Why sleep ye? rise and pray, lest ye enter into temptation.*

"RISE AND PRAY, LEST YE ENTER INTO TEMPTATION"

Twice in the garden, Jesus told His disciples to pray, lest they fall into temptation! Show me a fallen Christian, and I will show you a Christian who lacks in his prayer life!

Luke 23:31 *For if they do these things in a green tree, what shall be done in the dry?*

"WHAT SHALL BE DONE IN THE DRY"

The proverb here plainly means: "If such sufferings alight upon the innocent One, the very Lamb of God, what must be in store for those who are provoking the flames?" (Jamieson-Fausset-Brown)

Luke 24:38 *And he said unto them, Why are ye troubled? and why do thoughts arise in your hearts?*

"WHY ARE YE TROUBLED"

The disciples had seen the empty tomb! They had heard the account of the women at the tomb and what the angels had said! The two men that had seen Jesus on the road to Emmaus had returned and spoken of their encounter! Yet even as Jesus appeared to them, they thought Him to be a spirit! Why such lack of faith? Simply that they were living in a state of fear! A child of God will either walk in faith or in fear!

Luke 24:32 *And they said one to another, Did not our heart burn within us, while he talked with us by the way, and while he opened to us the scriptures?*

"DID NOT OUR HEART BURN WITHIN US"

How interesting that when Jesus spoke and opened the scriptures, those that heard were moved in their hearts. Too often, we come into God's house and hear the Word of God preached with no effect! What does that say about a heart that hears but is not moved?

GLEANINGS FROM THE BOOK OF JOHN

John 1:16 *And of his fulness have all we received, and grace for grace.*

"AND GRACE FOR GRACE"

A drop of God's grace would be sufficient in our time of need, but God does not stop there; rather, He gives us the fullness of His grace. We are overcome and completely engulfed with grace on top of grace!

John 3:19 *And this is the condemnation, that light is come into the world, and men loved darkness rather than light, because their deeds were evil.*

"AND MEN LOVED DARKNESS RATHER THAN LIGHT"

The reason church pews are empty on Sunday, the reason people reject the good news of salvation, is a simple one. If truth be told, people love darkness rather than light. To walk in light is to reveal one's faults and failures. To walk in light is to come clean. Walking in light gives us a clear path versus wandering in darkness and would result in the admission of one being lost.

John 6:17 *And entered into a ship, and went over the sea toward Capernaum. And it was now dark, and Jesus was not come to them.* **20** *But he saith unto them, It is I; be not afraid.*

"AND IT WAS NOW DARK, AND JESUS WAS NOT COME TO THEM"

Sometimes in our darkest hour, we assume Jesus is not there! If we will just be still and listen, we can hear Him whisper, "IT IS I; BE NOT AFRAID." The Creator of the wind and the rain knows how to still the storm!

John 7:7 *The world cannot hate you; but me it hateth, because I testify of it, that the works thereof are evil.*

"THE WORLD CANNOT HATE YOU; BUT ME IT HATETH"

A man can have a conversation about anything under the sun freely and openly, but as soon as the name Jesus is mentioned, all conversation comes to a halt! It is not the individual that the world hates, but rather it is Christ within and what He represents that the world hates. It is Christ who brings to light one's sinful lifestyle!

John 9:5 *As long as I am in the world, I am the light of the world.*

"AS LONG AS I AM IN THE WORLD"

Jesus, knowing that He was but a short while here on Earth, was a light to a darkened world! Life is but a vapor. We are not promised tomorrow. As Jesus was a light, so should we also be a light. Life is too short to waste on foolishness!

John 10:24 *Then came the Jews round about him, and said unto him, How long dost thou make us to doubt? If thou be the Christ, tell us plainly.*

"IF THOU BE THE CHRIST, TELL US PLAINLY"

Another example in scripture where people say one thing but really mean another. Jesus had plainly declared himself to be the Christ, but because it was not followed by lightning and thunder, they believed not. Though truth may sit right in front of you, if it is not wrapped up in pretty bows and ribbons, we choose oftentimes to ignore it. Let us be careful, for Satan himself is transformed into an angel of light!

John 12:43 *For they loved the praise of men more than the praise of God.*

"FOR THEY LOVED THE PRAISE OF MEN"

To receive accolades is a good thing, but just as the love of money is the root of all evil, so similarly is the love or desire of the praise of men. A Christian ought rather to seek God's approval than that of man!

John 15:8 *Herein is my Father glorified, that ye bear much fruit; so shall ye be my disciples.*

"THAT YE BEAR MUCH FRUIT"

That one bear fruit has a twofold purpose. Notice the first: that God is glorified! The second is that there may be evidence of being His disciples! Serving the Lord is glorifying to God! Let us bear fruit!

John 16:1 *These things have I spoken unto you, that ye should not be offended.*

"THAT YE SHOULD NOT BE OFFENDED"

Those who are offended easily tell on themselves. Jesus clearly told His disciples that they should not be offended because Christ had already warned them. The Christian who is offended easily does not know the scripture, the Word of God; for if we would but read His Word, then we would not be easily offended.

John 21:25 *And there are also many other things which Jesus did, the which, if they should be written every one, I suppose that even the world itself could not contain the books that should be written. Amen.*

"I SUPPOSE THAT EVEN THE WORLD ITSELF COULD NOT CONTAIN THE BOOKS THAT SHOULD BE WRITTEN. AMEN"

If everything were documented that Jesus did, there would not be enough paper to describe how great our Lord and Savior is! The world could not contain the volumes upon volumes of books that would be written, so says John!

GLEANINGS FROM THE BOOK OF ACTS

Acts 4:13 *Now when they saw the boldness of Peter and John, and perceived that they were unlearned and ignorant men, they marvelled, and they took knowledge of them, that they had been with Jesus.*

"NOW WHEN THEY SAW THE BOLDNESS OF PETER AND JOHN...THAT THEY HAD BEEN WITH JESUS"

Every soul that had an encounter with Jesus walked away a different person. It is impossible for someone to meet Jesus and keep it quiet! You will be known by who you associate with. One who is a true believer will be bold in their witness!

How interesting that what the world perceives as ignorant, God uses to His glory. God gave them boldness insomuch that men marveled and gave them respect, for their actions were such that they had been with Jesus!

Acts 5:28 *Saying, Did not we straitly command you that ye should not teach in this name? and, behold, ye have filled Jerusalem with your doctrine, and intend to bring this man's blood upon us.* **29** *Then Peter and the other apostles answered and said, We ought to obey God rather than men.*

"YE HAVE FILLED JERUSALEM WITH YOUR DOCTRINE"

"WE OUGHT TO OBEY GOD RATHER THAN MEN."

I have found often that teaching and preaching that the Word of God is not always popular or pleasant to the ear. Sharper than any two-edged sword, piercing and reaching to the very core of the cold and hardened heart. We could avoid such teaching, and yet, "we ought to obey God rather than men."

Acts 8:21 *Thou hast neither part nor lot in this matter: for thy heart is not right in the sight of God.*

"THOU HAST NEITHER PART NOR LOT IN THIS MATTER"

Simon the sorcerer had requested of Peter to endue him with the same power so that he too could heal the sick. Peter rebuked Simon, for he had no business doing magic tricks in the name of the Lord for a profit! And yet many a televangelist performs their tricks for monetary gain. Is it of God or is it sorcery?

Acts 8:23 *For I perceive that thou art in the gall of bitterness, and in the bond of iniquity.*

"AND IN THE BOND OF INIQUITY"

Simon the sorcerer tried to purchase the power of the Holy Spirit, even though he had claimed to have accepted Christ. Salvation cannot be purchased but is a free gift. Salvation cannot be earned by good works. Peter declared that though he had proclaimed to be saved, his actions declared something else. Not everyone who cries yea, yea, Lord, is truly saved!

Acts 10:28 *And he said unto them, Ye know how that it is an unlawful thing for a man that is a Jew to keep company, or come unto one of another nation; but God hath shewed me that I should not call any man common or unclean.*

"I SHOULD NOT CALL ANY MAN COMMON OR UNCLEAN"

Racism is a horrible thing, and God is no respecter of persons. It is not for us to judge between one class of people from another. Nor is it right for one to judge someone by the color of their skin. God hath said that all have sinned and come short of the glory of God. For God so loved the world that He gave His only begotten Son, that whosoever believeth might be saved!

Acts 11:23 *Who, when he came, and had seen the grace of God, was glad, and exhorted them all, that with purpose of heart they would cleave unto the Lord.*

"AND HAD SEEN THE GRACE OF GOD, WAS GLAD"

They were first called Christians at Antioch. The church grew and was prosperous. Barnabas was glad and gave encouragement. How often do we scoff and grumble when God pours His grace down on others. To grumble at others for God's blessing is to grumble at God Himself.

Acts 13:38 *Be it known unto you therefore, men and brethren, that through this man is preached unto you the forgiveness of sins:*

"THAT THROUGH THIS MAN IS PREACHED UNTO YOU THE FORGIVENESS OF SINS"

What do you preach? Many preach politics! Many preach a message of division amongst the brethren! Many preach their pet peeves on a soap box! Many preach false doctrines! Paul preached the forgiveness of sins! There is no greater message to be preached!

Acts 14:2 *But the unbelieving Jews stirred up the Gentiles, and made their minds evil affected against the brethren.*

"AND MADE THEIR MINDS EVIL EFFECTED AGAINST THE BRETHREN"

There is a spiritual battle that is ongoing, and it is a battle for the mind. The key to changing a society is to change how the people of that society think. One's actions always start with a thought process. If Satan can get a hold of your mind, then you will do evil on your own.

Acts 16:20 *And brought them to the magistrates, saying, These men, being Jews, do exceedingly trouble our city,* **21** *And teach customs, which are not lawful for us to receive, neither to observe, being Romans.*

"DO EXCEEDINGLY TROUBLE OUR CITY"

You will know when you have impacted your city when its MAGISTRATES or rulers accuse you of troubling their city! This is proof you are having an impact on your city. It is a great testimony to be accused of causing trouble for sharing the Gospel of Jesus Christ with your respective community. In the next chapter, they are accused of turning the world upside down. Oh, that there would be a man of God that would have such an impact!

Acts 17:6 *And when they found them not, they drew Jason and certain brethren unto the rulers of the city, crying, These that have turned the world upside down are come hither also;*

"THESE THAT HAVE TURNED THE WORLD UPSIDE DOWN ARE COME HITHER ALSO"

The disciples had a reputation of being men who turned the world upside down for the cause of Christ. There has been many a great preacher in our modern day, but none have had such passion as did the disciples! There could be no greater compliment from those in the world than to hear them say that the world has been turned upside down due to our witness for Christ!

Acts 21:13 *Then Paul answered, What mean ye to weep and to break mine heart? for I am ready not to be bound only, but also to die at Jerusalem for the name of the Lord Jesus.*

"WHAT MEAN YE TO WEEP AND TO BREAK MINE HEART"

Though the men meant well in discouraging Paul from going back to Jerusalem, it broke Paul's heart, for that was what he believed God wanted him to do. Many a good church member has broken the heart of a pastor with discouraging words!

The Jews would have killed Paul, and yet Paul was willing to go anyway. The fact that his friends tried to discourage him broke his heart. Oh, that we would have such conviction in that even death would not detour us from serving the Lord.

Acts 24:25 *And as he reasoned of righteousness, temperance, and judgment to come, Felix trembled, and answered, Go thy way for this time; when I have a convenient season, I will call for thee.*

"WHEN I HAVE A CONVENIENT SEASON, I WILL CALL FOR THEE"

Time is something none are guaranteed. As Paul shared Jesus, Felix trembled! Felix said he would listen at a more convenient time. Now is the time of salvation. Don't hesitate, for there is no guarantee of tomorrow!

Acts 26:2 *I think myself happy, king Agrippa, because I shall answer for myself this day before thee touching all the things whereof I am accused of the Jews:*

"I THINK MYSELF HAPPY"

Even though in captivity, bruised from previous beatings, and having been falsely accused, Paul chooses to be happy. Paul's joy came from his relationship with Christ. How often do we seek happiness in the things of this world only to be disappointed.

Acts 26:28 *Then Agrippa said unto Paul, Almost thou persuadest me to be a Christian.*

"ALMOST THOU PERSUADEST ME TO BE A CHRISTIAN"

Some of the saddest words in all of Scripture! Almost just doesn't cut it! There is many a soul in Hell who said that same word, ALMOST! You can have that assurance and know beyond a shadow of a doubt that Heaven is your home.

Acts 27:31 *Paul said to the centurion and to the soldiers, Except these abide in the ship, ye cannot be saved.*

"EXCEPT THESE ABIDE IN THE SHIP, YE CANNOT BE SAVED"

The ship of JESUS CHRIST! For it is by no other name that we are saved! Let us be busy about the Father's business and invite all that we meet to get on board the ship! The call to abandon ship would have resulted in many a man killed by the force of the waves throwing them against the rocks. Paul declared that there was safety in the ship! Many a lost soul is thrown into the oceans of life only to be thrown against the rocks of sin. Salvation is in Christ alone, for He is the ark of protection and none other!

GLEANINGS FROM THE BOOK OF ROMANS

Romans 1:8 *First, I thank my God through Jesus Christ for you all, that your faith is spoken of throughout the whole world.*

"THAT YOUR FAITH IS SPOKEN OF THROUGHOUT THE WHOLE WORLD"

Paul, writing to the church at Rome, makes a very profound statement when he says that their faith was known throughout the whole world! To be a follower of Christ in Rome would not be an easy thing. Likewise, in today's day and time, to be a follower of Christ is not a popular thing. Oh, to have such faith that it is known throughout the world!

Romans 1:16 *For I am not ashamed of the gospel of Christ: for it is the power of God unto salvation to every one that believeth; to the Jew first, and also to the Greek.*

"FOR IT IS THE POWER OF GOD"

It's a curious thing why so many would be ashamed of being in possession of a powerful thing. Not just any power but the greatest power. A power that can even raise the dead. A power that saves those that believe! If a person would hold such a power, you would think they would be braggadocious.

Romans 8:16 *The Spirit itself beareth witness with our spirit, that we are the children of God:*

"THE SPIRIT ITSELF BEARETH WITNESS WITH OUR SPIRIT"

The Holy Spirit has a very presence that cannot help but show forth. When an individual accepts Christ, the Holy Spirit indwells that individual and thus is reflected in that individual's everyday actions. Salvation is not gained by works but rather becomes evident through one's works!

Romans 8:18 *For I reckon that the sufferings of this present time are not worthy to be compared with the glory which shall be revealed in us.*

"THE SUFFERINGS OF THIS PRESENT TIME ARE NOT WORTHY TO BE COMPARED"

As the song writer put it, "It will be worth it all when we see Jesus. Life's trials will seem so small, when we see Christ!" As harsh as this present life can be, it will be overcome by the glory and majesty of our Lord and Savior! What a day that will be, when my Jesus I shall see, when I look upon His face, the One who saved me by His grace!

Romans 10:1 *Brethren, my heart's desire and prayer to God for Israel is, that they might be saved.*

"THAT THEY MIGHT BE SAVED"

Paul's HEART'S DESIRE and his PRAYER TO GOD was that the lost would come to the saving knowledge of Jesus Christ! Could it be that our prayer life is not what it should be because our heart is not where it should be?

Romans 10:18 *But I say, Have they not heard? Yes verily, their sound went into all the earth, and their words unto the ends of the world.*

"BUT I SAY, HAVE THEY NOT HEARD"

Have they not heard? Yes, all of Israel had heard but rejected the corner stone. Jesus became a stumbling block to the Jews. Verse twenty-one says, "All day long I have stretched forth my hands unto a disobedient and gainsaying people." It would appear that the United States of America has followed in the same manner.

Romans 12:3 *For I say, through the grace given unto me, to every man that is among you, not to think of himself more highly than he ought to think; but to think soberly, according as God hath dealt to every man the measure of faith.*

"FOR I SAY, THROUGH THE GRACE GIVEN UNTO ME"

The difference between men who speak with pride versus those who don't! The answer is grace. Paul spoke by the grace of God. The man who spews words of truth without grace is only drawing attention to himself!

Romans 13:14 *But put ye on the Lord Jesus Christ, and make not provision for the flesh, to fulfil the lusts thereof.*

"AND MAKE NOT PROVISION FOR THE FLESH"

In the words of John the Baptist, "He must increase, but I must decrease." We should put our fleshly desires aside that Christ might be magnified and glorified in us and through us! The psalmist wrote, "Thy word have I hid in mine heart, that I might not sin against thee."

GLEANINGS FROM THE BOOK OF
1 CORINTHIANS

1 Corinthians 1:9 *But we had the sentence of death in ourselves, that we should not trust in ourselves, but in God which raiseth the dead:*

"THAT WE SHOULD NOT TRUST IN OURSELVES"

The flesh is weak; we are to trust in the Lord with all our hearts and lean not on our own understanding. The One who can raise the dead can surely take care of our earthly trials and tribulations.

---

1 Corinthians 3:3 *For ye are yet carnal: for whereas there is among you envying, and strife, and divisions, are ye not carnal, and walk as men?*

"FOR YE ARE YET CARNAL"

Paul rebukes the church at Corinth with a harsh criticism, calling them carnal, for they were full of envy, strife, and divisions. In other words, God's people were seeking after their own fleshy desires. These things are the outward evidence of a carnal life! There will be unity amongst God's people, but there will be divisiveness amongst carnal Christians.

---

1 Corinthians 3:6 *I have planted, Apollos watered; but God gave the increase.*

"BUT GOD GAVE THE INCREASE"

Using the example of a farmer, Paul tells us that we are simply tools in the Master's hand! We have no power within us to make anything grow! We must simply be obedient and plant the seed. God will give the increase in His time! Don't quit! Stay faithful in His fields, plant those seeds, water, and care for it, for God will give the increase!

1 Corinthians 3:10 *According to the grace of God which is given unto me, as a wise master builder, I have laid the foundation, and another buildeth thereon. But let every man take heed how he buildeth thereupon.*

"BUT LET EVERY MAN TAKE HEED HOW HE BUILDETH THEREUPON"

Interesting thought presented by Paul. The importance of a foundation and, even more so, how one builds upon that foundation. How often does a man come behind another and tear down what has been established? How does this accomplish anything? Rather it creates an endless cycle of building up just see it torn down!

---

1 Corinthians 8:9 *But take heed lest by any means this liberty of yours become a stumbling block to them that are weak.*

"THIS LIBERTY OF YOURS BECOME A STUMBLING BLOCK TO THEM THAT ARE WEAK"

There are many things in life that some would call a gray area. They are things not clearly stated in scripture as to whether or not they are sin. Christian liberty, it is so called. It's not hurting anyone, so it must be okay to do. Paul's rebuke is not in regard to right or wrong; but rather, will the liberty that we express hinder someone from accepting Christ? If so, then Christian liberty in and of itself is sin.

---

1 Corinthians 8:11 *And through thy knowledge shall the weak brother perish, for whom Christ died?*

"AND THROUGH THY KNOWLEDGE SHALL THE WEAK BROTHER PERISH"

The gray areas, or are they really gray? For everything in scripture is black and white, right or wrong. In and of itself, the eating of meat is not wrong, but taking part in idolatry is obviously sin. Therefore, if eating meat that has been in a pagan ceremony should cause one to stumble or draw them away from Christ, then we are to abstain.

---

1 Corinthians 10:21 *Ye cannot drink the cup of the Lord, and the cup of devils: ye cannot be partakers of the Lord's table, and of the table of devils.*

"YE CANNOT BE PARTAKERS OF THE LORDS TABLE, AND OF THE TABLE OF DEVILS"

Let us consider all of our actions, for all that we do is either to the glory of one or the other! Whose table will you dine at today? The Lord's or the Devil's?

---

1 Corinthians 12:3 *Wherefore I give you to understand, that no man speaking by the Spirit of God calleth Jesus accursed: and that no man can say that Jesus is the Lord, but by the Holy Ghost.*

"AND THAT NO MAN CAN SAY THAT JESUS IS THE LORD, BUT BY THE HOLY GHOST"

There are many who proclaim Christ but yet cannot truly say they know Christ, for the Holy Spirit will proclaim Christ by His own character. Thus the reason so many proclaim but their life does not reflect what they speak.

---

1 Corinthians 15:19 *If in this life only we have hope in Christ, we are of all men most miserable.*

"WE ARE OF ALL MEN MOST MISERABLE"

Truth be told, a man without Christ is a miserable man! Let us not be fooled by ones outward appearance, for a smile could be nothing but a facade to disguise a lack of peace inside!

GLEANINGS FROM THE BOOK OF
2 CORINTHIANS

2 Corinthians 1:4 *Who comforteth us in all our tribulation, that we may be able to comfort them which are in any trouble, by the comfort wherewith we ourselves are comforted of God.*

"THAT WE MAY BE ABLE TO COMFORT THEM WHICH ARE IN ANY TROUBLE"

The past is preparation for our future! God many times allows us to endure heartache so that through that experience, we might be able to comfort someone down the road. Not just with good words and deeds, but by sharing with them Jesus, the One in Whom we found our comfort!

---

2 Corinthians 1:6 *And whether we be afflicted, it is for your consolation and salvation, which is effectual in the enduring of the same sufferings which we also suffer: or whether we be comforted, it is for your consolation and salvation.*

"AND WHETHER WE BE AFFLICTED, IT IS FOR YOUR CONSOLATION AND SALVATION"

It's interesting that Paul would say that his afflictions were to the benefit of others! First, having gone through an affliction, we are the better qualified to help others going through the same affliction. Second, how we handle those afflictions are a witness and testimony to those around us! Your affliction could be used to reach others! Trials, tribulations, and afflictions are often, at least from our view point anyway, a time for us to sink into discouragement; however, it is in those times that God can use us to encourage others and even see others come to Christ!

---

2 Corinthians 6:1 *We then, as workers together with him, beseech you also that ye receive not the grace of God in vain.*

"THAT YE RECEIVE NOT THE GRACE OF GOD IN VAIN"

The very next verse declares that we have been wonderfully saved. The following handful of verses declare all the trials and tribulations that one may encounter in the ministry, and yet there should be no offense taken. If we are offended, then we are declaring the grace of God to be in vain. To take on the ministry is to accept affliction, and yet we are to find peace in our salvation.

---

2 Corinthians 7:10 *For godly sorrow worketh repentance to salvation not to be repented of: but the sorrow of the world worketh death.*

"BUT THE SORROW OF THE WORLD WORKETH DEATH"

Sorrow that comes from repentance is covered in grace and mercy. Sorrow without repentance as a result of self-inflicted sin is simply grief to the grave.

---

2 Corinthians 8:2 *How that in a great trial of affliction the abundance of their joy and their deep poverty abounded unto the riches of their liberality.*

"THE ABUNDANCE OF THEIR JOY"

Often, the church at Macedonia is used as an example of their generous giving even during a time of affliction and poverty. We miss, however, the fact that even during these times of poverty and afflictions, they had an abundance of joy. We will have no problem staying faithful during times of affliction and poverty if we will but rely on the Lord to bring us joy.

---

2 Corinthians 8:3 *For to their power, I bear record, yea, and beyond their power they were willing of themselves;*

"YEA, AND BEYOND THEIR POWER THEY WERE WILLING OF THEMSELVES"

God is not asking us to do what we cannot bear but rather simply asking that we be willing to be obedient to His calling! God will respond to our willingness, and then we will see great and mighty works beyond our physical capabilities!

---

2 Corinthians 10:7 *Do ye look on things after the outward appearance? If any man trust to himself that he is Christ's, let him of himself think this again, that, as he is Christ's, even so are we Christ's.*

"DO YE LOOK ON THINGS AFTER THE OUTWARD APPEARANCE"

Not everyone who claims to be a Christian is. Be careful of the outward appearance of a Christian, for the true evidence of a Christian is not the clothes they wear or flowery speech but rather if they produce fruit.

---

2 Corinthians 12:10 *Therefore I take pleasure in infirmities, in reproaches, in necessities, in persecutions, in distresses for Christ's sake: for when I am weak, then am I strong.*

"FOR WHEN I AM WEAK, THEN AM I STRONG"

There is an old saying that says, "Whatever doesn't kill you will only make you stronger." No doubt that this is not true physically, but spiritually, it should strengthen our awareness and knowledge as well as discernment. We are now better equipped to handle a situation should it arise again. Even more so, we now carry the tools spiritually to help and guide others as they endure the same trial.

GLEANINGS FROM THE BOOK OF GALATIANS

Galatians 1:6 *I marvel that ye are so soon removed from him that called you into the grace of Christ unto another gospel:*

"I MARVEL THAT YE ARE SO SOON REMOVED FROM HIM"

I also, like Paul, am amazed at how quickly those who claim to be Christians are so quickly removed from truth and submit themselves to false teaching. Oh, how we wear our feelings on our sleeves. The walk of a Christian is not one of feelings; but rather, it is one of assurance!

Galatians 4:9 *But now, after that ye have known God, or rather are known of God, how turn ye again to the weak and beggarly elements, whereunto ye desire again to be in bondage?*

"OR RATHER ARE KNOWN OF GOD"

It is one thing to say that you know God, but the ultimate question is, does God know you? Even the demons acknowledge Christ for who He is. Having knowledge of who someone is and being part of their family circle are two different things.

Galatians 5:19 *Now the works of the flesh are manifest, which are these; Adultery, fornication, uncleanness, lasciviousness,*

"NOW THE WORKS OF THE FLESH ARE MANIFEST"

What is in you is what will come out. The real question is what will come out of the flesh or of the spirit. Though one may proclaim to be a Christian, their actions may prove otherwise.

Galatians 6:9 *And let us not be weary in well doing: for in due season we shall reap, if we faint not.*

"AND LET US NOT BE WEARY"

A recipe for success!
1. In whatever we do, let us be our best! (Well doing)
2. Success takes time! (For in due season)
3. There is a reward for hard work! (We shall reap)
4. Don't quit! (If we faint not)

GLEANINGS FROM THE BOOK OF EPHESIANS

Ephesians 1:13 *In whom ye also trusted, after that ye heard the word of truth, the gospel of your salvation: in whom also after that ye believed, ye were sealed with that holy Spirit of promise,*

"YE WERE SEALED WITH THAT HOLY SPIRIT OF PROMISE"

The gift of eternal salvation is the greatest of all gifts! For I am sealed with and by the Holy Spirit. Nothing can remove me from His hand. I can walk through this life with confidence, knowing that my eternity is secure!

Ephesians 2:13 *But now in Christ Jesus ye who sometimes were far off are made nigh by the blood of Christ.*

"MADE NIGH BY THE BLOOD OF CHRIST"

How often do we take for granted what has actually been done to save us from an eternity in Hell. The richness of His grace, the power of the Holy Spirit and the hope of eternity with Him. We are given so much spiritual wealth and yet live in spiritual poverty!

Ephesians 3:15 *Of whom the whole family in heaven and earth is named,*

"THE WHOLE FAMILY IN HEAVEN AND EARTH"

For those that are saved, there is a new name awaiting you. Just as the bride changes her name on her wedding day, so we are the bride of Christ and we are named after Christ!

Ephesians 3:20 *Now unto him that is able to do exceeding abundantly above all that we ask or think, according to the power that worketh in us,*

"NOW UNTO HIM THAT IS ABLE TO DO EXCEEDING ABUNDANTLY ABOVE ALL THAT WE ASK OR THINK"

How petty are the requests of man compared to what God is actually capable of doing. God can exceed all that we ask and can give over and above anything we ever could have imagined. Is anything too hard for God?

GLEANINGS FROM THE BOOK OF PHILIPPIANS

Philippians 1:8 *For God is my record, how greatly I long after you all in the bowels of Jesus Christ.*

"FOR GOD IS MY RECORD"

As Christians, we declare that we are a witness for the cause of Christ. Paul declared that God was his witness. An interesting thought. What does God think of our Christianity? If God were to be called to be a witness at our trial, what would our record show?

Philippians 4:3 *And I intreat thee also, true yokefellow, help those women which laboured with me in the gospel, with Clement also, and with other my fellowlabourers, whose names are in the book of life.*

"HELP THOSE WOMEN WHICH LABOURED WITH ME IN THE GOSPEL"

The power of praying women. It was Lydia in Acts 16 who opened her home to care for Paul and Silas. It was in her home that prayer meetings took place. It was Lydia who was the first convert in Paul's ministry in Europe. The gospel was spread throughout Europe because of a group of women who served faithfully and prayed earnestly. Such is the power of a Godly praying woman.

GLEANINGS FROM THE BOOK OF COLOSSIANS

Colossians 2:8 *Beware lest any man spoil you through philosophy and vain deceit, after the tradition of men, after the rudiments of the world, and not after Christ.*

"BEWARE LEST ANY MAN SPOIL YOU THROUGH PHILOSOPHY AND VAIN DECEIT, AFTER THE TRADITION OF MEN"

A warning is given to beware of true doctrine being spoiled by the philosophy of men. Many follow men and man's philosophy rather than God. We are to study to show ourselves approved unto God, not man.

Colossians 2:19 *For what is our hope, or joy, or crown of rejoicing? Are not even ye in the presence of our Lord Jesus Christ at his coming?*

"WHAT IS OUR HOPE, OR JOY, OR CROWN OF REJOICING"

For all that this world has to offer and all of its worldly pleasures, none of them will compare to the joy and rejoicing that we will experience when our hope is revealed in the person of Jesus Christ.

Colossians 4:6 *Let your speech be always with grace, seasoned with salt, that ye may know how ye ought to answer every man.*

"LET YOUR SPEECH BE ALWAYS WITH GRACE"

We are to speak the truth in love. Though we speak truth, it is often laced with anger and brutishness. Truth must always be delivered with grace.

GLEANINGS FROM THE BOOK OF
1 THESSALONIANS

1 Thessalonians 1:2 *We give thanks to God always for you all, making mention of you in our prayers;*

"MAKING MENTION OF YOU IN OUR PRAYERS"

More often than not, our prayers are selfish ones, We take our cares, our troubles, and our trials and lay them at the feet of Jesus. We rejoice in all that God has done in our lives. How often in our time of prayer do we rejoice for others? Whom did you pray for today?

---

1 Thessalonians 1:8 *For from you sounded out the word of the Lord not only in Macedonia and Achaia, but also in every place your faith to God-ward is spread abroad; so that we need not to speak any thing.*

"SO THAT WE NEED NOT TO SPEAK ANY THING"

This small church in Thessalonica, though having endured the same trials and suffering as the church at Macedonia, were so bold in their testimony that the church's testimony and message of salvation spread quicker than Paul could preach. Oh, that our churches were so bold that the pastor could say nothing and the Gospel could stil be spread throughout the world.

---

1 Thessalonians 2:10 *Ye are witnesses, and God also, how holily and justly and unblameably we behaved ourselves among you that believe:*

"HOW HOLILY AND JUSTLY AND UNBLAMEABLY WE BEHAVED OURSELVES"

People are watching you all the time, everyday. If your speech does not line up with your actions, then no one will take you seriously when it comes to sharing the Gospel of Christ.

1 Thessalonians 4:11 *And that ye study to be quiet, and to do your own business, and to work with your own hands, as we commanded you;*

"AND TO WORK WITH YOUR OWN HANDS, AS WE COMMANDED YOU"

Busybodies is a term used in Scripture to describe someone who has little to do other than to involve themselves in other people's business. Jesus Himself stated that He should be busy about His Father's business. Paul gives great counsel in that we all have our own calling; therefore, let us be attentive towards that which we have been called to do.

---

1 Thessalonians 5:22 *Abstain from all appearance of evil.* **23**. *And the very God of peace sanctify you wholly; and I pray God your whole spirit and soul and body be preserved blameless unto the coming of our Lord Jesus Christ.*

"ABSTAIN FROM ALL APPEARANCE OF EVIL"

On this day, October 31, can we say that we are abstaining from the appearance of evil? If the Lord were to return today, how would He find us? Blameless?

GLEANINGS FROM THE BOOK OF
2 THESSALONIANS

2 Thessalonians 1:6 *Seeing it is a righteous thing with God to recompense tribulation to them that trouble you;*

"SEEING IT IS A RIGHTEOUS THING WITH GOD TO RECOMPENSE TRIBULATION"

Paul's second letter to the church at Thessalonica, a church that endured many struggles and trials. Paul encourages the church to not quit, for the trial is all part of God's plan unto righteousness; the very ones that were afflicting the church would now be afflicted by God Himself. God will always bless faithfulness.

---

2 Thessalonians 2:13 *But we are bound to give thanks alway to God for you, brethren beloved of the Lord, because God hath from the beginning chosen you to salvation through sanctification of the Spirit and belief of the truth:*

"BECAUSE GOD HATH FROM THE BEGINNING CHOSEN YOU TO SALVATION"

God's plan from the beginning was to draw all men unto Him. The Holy Spirit draws men to Him. God does not send anyone to Hell; but rather, it is man's choice to deny the truth.

GLEANINGS FROM THE BOOK OF 1TIMOTHY

1 Timothy 2:1 *I exhort therefore, that, first of all, supplications, prayers, intercessions, and giving of thanks, be made for all men;* **2** *For kings, and for all that are in authority; that we may lead a quiet and peaceable life in all godliness and honesty.* **3** *For this is good and acceptable in the sight of God our Saviour;*

"THAT WE MAY LEAD A QUIET AND PEACEABLE LIFE IN ALL GODLINESS AND HONESTY"

The prayer life of a Christian should always include the lifting up of our leaders. We should pray for our local leaders just as well as our President, whomever he or she may be, no matter what political affiliation, so that we may lead a quiet and peaceable life!
In a world full of wars and rumors of wars, could there be a solution? Could we live a life of peace and godliness without fear? The reason so many Christians live a life of fear is simply a lack of prayer. Specifically, prayer for our world leaders. The solution for living a life of peace is simply prayer.

---

1 Timothy 2:8 *I will therefore that men pray everywhere, lifting up holy hands, without wrath and doubting.*

"WITHOUT WRATH AND DOUBTING"

The importance of prayer in the Christian life is a vital part of our personal relationship with God. With that in mind, the attitude we carry into prayer is equally important. Our spirit should not be one of anger and doubting but rather one of humility and faith.

---

1 Timothy 6:11 *But thou, O man of God, flee these things; and follow after righteousness, godliness, faith, love, patience, meekness.*

"AND FOLLOW AFTER RIGHTEOUSNESS, GODLINESS, FAITH, LOVE, PATIENCE, MEEKNESS"

A man of God is to follow after certain things. We pride ourselves in the following after of righteousness, Godliness and faith! It is, however, the latter half that too many a man of God desperately fails at. Love, patience, and meekness. The latter three are the outward expression of the first!

GLEANINGS FROM THE BOOK OF 2 TIMOTHY

2 Timothy 1:16 *The Lord give mercy unto the house of Onesiphorus; for he oft refreshed me, and was not ashamed of my chain:*

"AND WAS NOT ASHAMED OF MY CHAIN"

Paul was imprisoned for preaching the Gospel of Jesus Christ. Demas had forsaken him, but Onesiphorus was faithful to minister to him even while in chains. Thank you, Lord, for people who minister to the man of God unashamed!

---

2 Timothy 2:3 *Thou therefore endure hardness, as a good soldier of Jesus Christ. 4 No man that warreth entangleth himself with the affairs of this life; that he may please him who hath chosen him to be a soldier.*

"AS A GOOD SOLDIER OF JESUS CHRIST"

A good soldier is one who is tough, not a whiner and a crybaby. In the spiritual realm, a good soldier is one who does not allow the cares of this life to discourage or bring him down.

---

2 Timothy 2:13 *If we believe not, yet he abideth faithful: he cannot deny himself.*

"IF WE BELIEVE NOT, YET HE ABIDETH FAITHFUL"

How wonderful this verse is! When we lack in faith, we literally deny who He is and what He is able to do for us! Though our faith fails, yet He remains faithful to us!

---

2 Timothy 4:2 *Preach the word; be instant in season, out of season; reprove, rebuke, exhort with all longsuffering and doctrine.* **3** *For the time will come when they will not endure sound doctrine; but after their own lusts shall they heap to themselves teachers, having itching ears;*

"FOR THE TIME WILL COME"

There is coming a day when the trumpet shall sound, and we shall be caught up to meet Him in the air. Those that remain will believe lies. Time is running short. Let us be diligent to preach and share the gospel with everyone we meet.

GLEANINGS FROM THE BOOK OF TITUS

Titus 2:1 *But speak thou the things which become sound doctrine:*

"WHICH BECOME SOUND DOCTRINE"

Perhaps more easily understood is that we are to be careful to speak that which is fit for teaching. Is what comes out of our mouth uplifting and edifying to the hearer? Do we build up those around us, or do we break others down around us with the words we say?

GLEANINGS FROM THE BOOK OF HEBREWS

Hebrews 2:3 *How shall we escape, if we neglect so great salvation; which at the first began to be spoken by the Lord, and was confirmed unto us by them that heard him;*

"IF WE NEGLECT SO GREAT SALVATION"

Our salvation is not just any salvation, but oh, how great it is. The very act by which we have gained salvation through Christ's death is great. The debt owed, now paid in full, is great. The eternal security and hope of Heaven is great. Let us not neglect the sharing of such a great salvation.

How is it that people reject salvation? From the beginning of creation, even the angels declare Christ as Lord. Jesus's ministry and miracles declare Him to be Lord, and even now, we have a choice to make. We must choose salvation or decline His invitation. How can we neglect so great a salvation?

Hebrews 6:18 *That by two immutable things, in which it was impossible for God to lie, we might have a strong consolation, who have fled for refuge to lay hold upon the hope set before us:*

"THAT BY TWO IMMUTABLE THINGS, IN WHICH IT WAS IMPOSSIBLE FOR GOD TO LIE"

God cannot lie! It is an impossible thing! It has not, cannot, nor will ever happen. There are two things that never change. Number one is the promises of God. Two, simply the very Word of God! When God makes a promise, He will be true to that promise, for He cannot lie! Likewise, the Word of God is true and unchanging!

Hebrews 10:31 *It is a fearful thing to fall into the hands of the living God.*

"IT IS A FEARFUL THING TO FALL INTO THE HANDS OF THE LIVING GOD"

In today's society, there is a lack of fear. People ought to fear God! This selfish world that we live in seeks only to please itself with no concern as to one's actions towards others. To fall into the hands of a living God is something men ought to fear!

Hebrews 13:14 *For here have we no continuing city, but we seek one to come.*

"FOR WE HAVE NO CONTINUING CITY"

As the old saying goes, "There's no place like home." There does not seem to be a more comfortable place than one's own bed. The trials of this world will continue to plague us until we truly make it home to Heaven.

GLEANINGS FROM THE BOOK OF JAMES

James 1:26 *If any man among you seem to be religious, and bridleth not his tongue, but deceiveth his own heart, this man's religion is vain.*

"BUT DECEIVETH HIS OWN HEART, THIS MAN'S RELIGION IS VAIN"

In a world driven by social media, there is a great urge among Christians to prove their knowledge and wisdom in open forums. James is quite clear that there are people who cannot bridle their tongue. What comes out of one's mouth is the truth behind one's soul. Though someone declares themself to be a religious person and yet cannot control their tongue, they but deceive themselves. For blessing and cursing cannot come from the same mouth. He is either one or the other, for they deceive their own heart and their display of religion is in vain! Actions truly speak louder than words!

James 3:2 *For in many things we offend all. If any man offend not in word, the same is a perfect man, and able also to bridle the whole body.*

"AND ABLE ALSO TO BRIDLE THE WHOLE BODY"

The theme of the book of James is faith. The spiritually mature Christian who walks in faith will show some character traits of his faith. One of those traits is a bridled tongue. Many a Christian will speak out of line rather than slow down and allow God to speak through them.

James 3:5 *Even so the tongue is a little member, and boasteth great things. Behold, how great a matter a little fire kindleth!* **6** *And the tongue is a fire, a world of iniquity: so is the tongue among our members, that it defileth the whole body, and setteth on fire the course of nature; and it is set on fire of hell.*

"AND SETTETH ON FIRE THE COURSE OF NATURE"

Let our mouths be used for the glory of God! Be careful what you say today, for it will set a course! Either it will enrage the fires of HELL or ring the bells of HEAVEN!

James 5:8 *Be ye also patient; stablish your hearts: for the coming of the Lord draweth nigh.*

"BE YE ALSO PATIENT"

Though we know not the day or hour our Lord will come, we ought to anticipate His coming. Through preparation and patience, we look for His coming. Daily we ought to prepare our hearts and be looking and listening for the sound of the trumpet.

GLEANINGS FROM THE BOOK OF 1 PETER

1Peter 1:12 *Unto whom it was revealed, that not unto themselves, but unto us they did minister the things, which are now reported unto you by them that have preached the gospel unto you with the Holy Ghost sent down from heaven; which things the angels desire to look into.*

"WHICH THINGS THE ANGELS DESIRE TO LOOK INTO"

God has given us the power to do something that even the angels can't do. As powerful as the angels are, even to overthrow demonic forces, they, however, have not been given this ability. Only we have been given the power of the Holy Spirit, both to preach and to grow in grace.

---

1 Peter 3:21 *The like figure whereunto even baptism doth also now save us (not the putting away of the filth of the flesh, but the answer of a good conscience toward God,) by the resurrection of Jesus Christ:*

"THE LIKE FIGURE WHEREUNTO EVEN BAPTISM DOTH ALSO NOW SAVE US"

The like figure, or just like Noah in the previous verse. As the floodwaters destroyed the filth of the earth and lifted up the ark holding the remnant of Salvation, so does baptism lift up and support the remnant of the saved in Christ! Not salvation in the water but "the like figure:" a picture, if you will, of Salvation.

GLEANINGS FROM THE BOOK OF 2 PETER

2 Peter 1:5 *And beside this, giving all diligence, add to your faith virtue; and to virtue knowledge;* **6** *And to knowledge temperance; and to temperance patience; and to patience godliness;* **7** *And to godliness brotherly kindness; and to brotherly kindness charity.*

"ADD TO YOUR FAITH VIRTUE"

The true evidence of Godliness is a loving Spirit. It is one thing to say that we have faith, but true faith is manifested in love.

---

2 Peter 1:9 *But he that lacketh these things is blind, and cannot see afar off, and hath forgotten that he was purged from his old sins.*

"IS BLIND, AND CANNOT SEE AFAR OFF, AND HATH FORGOTTEN"

When you accepted Christ, you gained the power and ability to bear fruit. The Christian who does not, however, is blind and cannot comprehend the future hope we have in Christ. Not only are we blinded to the future, but we fail to remember what Christ has done for us on the cross. Therefore, the opposite is true; if we remember the price that was paid on Calvary for us so that we may have hope in a future eternal, we will desire to bear fruit.

---

2 Peter 2:17 *These are wells without water, clouds that are carried with a tempest; to whom the mist of darkness is reserved for ever.*

"THESE ARE WELLS WITHOUT WATER"

When Jesus met the Samaritan woman at the well, He offered her living water. On the contrary, a false teacher leads people to wells with no water. Their words are luring and seductive but leave the hearer empty and thirsting for truth. The true test of truth is the Word of God. Let us always be cautious of what we hear, for it may just be an empty well.

GLEANINGS FROM THE BOOKS OF 1st, 2nd, and 3rd JOHN

1 John 2:4 *He that saith, I know him, and keepeth not his commandments, is a liar, and the truth is not in him.*

"AND THE TRUTH IS NOT IN HIM"

What is in your heart is that which is revealed for all to see! If Christ is in you, then it will show! One who claims to know Christ and yet whose life does not reflect that of HIS commandments...IS A LIAR!

---

1 John 2:20 *But ye have an unction from the Holy One, and ye know all things.*

"BUT YE HAVE AN UNCTION FROM THE HOLY ONE"

We have an anointing from the Holy Ghost. When a person was anointed to be king, it declared them to be royalty even before they sat on the throne. We, likewise, have an unction which declares us to be children of the King of Kings and Lord of Lords, and therefore we have the power and authority to fight off the powers of darkness.

---

1 John 2:22 *Who is a liar but he that denieth that Jesus is the Christ? He is antichrist, that denieth the Father and the Son.*

"WHO IS A LIAR BUT HE THAT DENIETH THAT JESUS IS THE CHRIST"

Who are the liars of this world? Man cannot serve two masters. He will love the one and hate the other. Jesus said, "I am the way, the truth, and the life!" To deny Christ is to adhere to Satan. Satan is the father of lies! To deny Christ is to deny truth; therefore, you adhere to lies and you yourself are a liar!

1 John 3:16 *Hereby perceive we the love of God, because he laid down his life for us: and we ought to lay down our lives for the brethren.* **17** *But whoso hath this world's good, and seeth his brother have need, and shutteth up his bowels of compassion from him, how dwelleth the love of God in him?*

"AND WE OUGHT TO LAY DOWN OUR LIVES FOR THE BRETHREN"

You would think that the attitude of a born-again Christian towards other Christians would be civil; however, the disputing amongst Christians is no new thing. When the true love of God is displayed in us, there is a spirit of giving oneself for another. Even unto death!

---

1 John 4:10 *Herein is love, not that we loved God, but that he loved us, and sent his Son to be the propitiation for our sins.*

"NOT THAT WE LOVED GOD, BUT THAT HE LOVED US"

True and perfect love is that God loves us. God is love. Loving is a natural response from God. It is perfect love in every way. We, on the other, hand have to force ourselves to love and commit and strive to love one another. Thus, there is no greater love so much so that He gave His only begotten Son to die for our sins!

2 John 1:10 *If there come any unto you, and bring not this doctrine, receive him not into your house, neither bid him God speed:*

"NEITHER BID HIM GOD SPEED"

Often, one's own home would be the meeting place for people to gather and fellowship around the Word of God. In regard to the preaching and teaching of God's Word, we are to be cautious of who we allow to present that message. One who would not carry the same doctrine should not be received, nor should they be encouraged to present their false message to others.

---

3 John 1:4 *I have no greater joy than to hear that my children walk in truth.*

"MY CHILDREN WALK IN TRUTH"

A man's heritage is in his children. Not an inheritance of riches or gold but to raise up Godly Christian children. If men of God instill the Word of God upon the hearts of His children, then it is a true statement that the grass withers and the flower fades, but the Word of God will stand forever. Forever in the hearts of His children.

GLEANINGS FROM THE BOOK OF JUDE

Jude 1:4 *For there are certain men crept in unawares, who were before of old ordained to this condemnation, ungodly men, turning the grace of our God into lasciviousness, and denying the only Lord God, and our Lord Jesus Christ.*

"UNGODLY MEN TURNING THE GRACE OF OUR GOD INTO LASCIVIOUSNESS"

There are those who call themselves pastors who are simply using the ministry for fleshly gain, using the grace of God as a cover for criminal and ungodly behavior. Such men are not true followers of Christ but rather deny Him in their selfish actions!

Jude 1:8 *Likewise also these filthy dreamers defile the flesh, despise dominion, and speak evil of dignities.*

"LIKEWISE ALSO THESE FILTHY DREAMERS DEFILE THE FLESH"

Something that sounds good but has no truth to it. A false doctrine made up and presented as truth. A lifestyle of filth and a doctrine made up in fantasy land. This is the false narrative and lifestyle of a heretic!

Jude 1:22 *And of some have compassion, making a difference:*

"AND OF SOME HAVE COMPASSION"

Difference makers are people of compassion!

GLEANINGS FROM THE BOOK OF REVELATION

Revelation 1:1 *The Revelation of Jesus Christ, which God gave unto him, to shew unto his servants things which must shortly come to pass; and he sent and signified it by his angel unto his servant John: 2 Who bare record of the word of God, and of the testimony of Jesus Christ, and of all things that he saw. 3 Blessed is he that readeth, and they that hear the words of this prophecy, and keep those things which are written therein: for the time is at hand.*

"THE REVELATION OF JESUS CHRIST"

Though the book of Revelation is certainly prophetic, we often overlook the theme and purpose of the book of Revelation. The book itself is Christ revealing Himself to the world. What has been preached and taught for over three thousand years will be revealed. Christ's power and glory will be revealed for all to see. All who read and look forward to His revealing are blessed! Lord, come quickly!

Revelation 1:18 *I am he that liveth, and was dead; and, behold, I am alive for evermore, Amen; and have the keys of hell and of death.*

"I AM HE THAT LIVETH, AND WAS DEAD; AND, BEHOLD, I AM ALIVE FOR EVERMORE, AMEN"

Jesus Christ was born of a virgin, lived thirty three and a half years, was crucified, died and was buried, then rose again on the third day! It is this same Jesus that is surrounded by angels in Heaven who proclaim, "HOLY, HOLY, HOLY IS THE LAMB THAT WAS SLAIN!" He was and He is and forever shall be "ALIVE FOR EVERMORE, AMEN!"

Revelation 2:4 *Nevertheless I have somewhat against thee, because thou hast left thy first love.*

"BECAUSE THOU HAST LEFT THY FIRST LOVE"

The history of the church laid out over the first three chapters of Revelation. At the end of chapter three, we see the lukewarm church of Laodicea. A church so vile that it is nauseating in Gods eyes and spewed out! How does the church get to such a point in history? It started in the early era of the church at Ephesus when they left their first love. A backslidden church can always retrace their steps back to where they lost their love for the things of God!

Revelation 2:9 *I know thy works, and tribulation, and poverty, (but thou art rich) and I know the blasphemy of them which say they are Jews, and are not, but are the synagogue of Satan.*

"BUT ARE THE SYNAGOGUE OF SATAN"

The synagogue was the place of gathering for the Jews, a place where they were to sit under good, fundamental teaching. There were Jews sitting amongst their brethren, all the while having an evil spirit about them. This same spirit that cried "crucify him" would gather in the synagogue with the masses. The same spirit exist even in today's church. There seems to always be someone who would disrupt, criticize, and dismantle what the man of God is trying to establish. Satan's patrons sit in the pews of the church.

Revelation 2:16 *Repent; or else I will come unto thee quickly, and will fight against them with the sword of my mouth.*

"AND WILL FIGHT AGAINST THEM WITH THE SWORD OF MY MOUTH"

Just as the world was created by His spoken Word, so will the final battle of the ages be won with but His spoken Word. No swords, guns, or weapon of any type will be needed. His spoken Word will be enough.

Revelation 5:5 *And one of the elders saith unto me, Weep not: behold, the Lion of the tribe of Juda, the Root of David, hath prevailed to open the book, and to loose the seven seals thereof.* **9** *And they sung a new song, saying, Thou art worthy to take the book, and to open the seals thereof: for thou wast slain, and hast redeemed us to God by thy blood out of every kindred, and tongue, and people, and nation;*

"THOU ART WORTHY TO TAKE THE BOOK"

The day will come when evil will be rewarded with judgment from Heaven's throne. Seven seals will be opened, and those seven seals will unleash death and destruction upon this earth. Who is worthy to conquer such evil? Not Christians, for we have been delivered from such evil; but rather, the Lamb that was slain, who has already conquered sin and death. Jesus Himself is only worthy, and He alone will pass judgment upon this earth.

Revelation 8:4 *And the smoke of the incense, which came with the prayers of the saints, ascended up before God out of the angel's hand.*

"WHICH CAME WITH THE PRAYERS OF THE SAINTS"

In the midst of the great tribulation, God is still hearing prayers. The cares of this world today are nothing compared to what those who are alive during the great tribulation will experience. How comforting it is to know that our prayers ascend up into Heaven and reach the throne room of God Himself.

Revelation 12:7 *And there was war in heaven: Michael and his angels fought against the dragon; and the dragon fought and his angels*

"AND THERE WAS WAR IN HEAVEN"

Not in the throne room of God, for that had long been settled when Satan and a third of Heaven were thrown to the earth. This is an all-out spiritual dual between Michael and his army versus demonic forces! Oh, if we had the ability to see into the spirit world! For we wrestle not against flesh and blood but rather against principalities and powers of darkness. A battle cry will ring out in heaven, and angelic forces will charge the demonic powers of Hell and will clash in midair!

Revelation 18:13 *And cinnamon, and odours, and ointments, and frankincense, and wine, and oil, and fine flour, and wheat, and beasts, and sheep, and horses, and chariots, and slaves, and souls of men.* **14** *And the fruits that thy soul lusted after are departed from thee, and all things which were dainty and goodly are departed from thee, and thou shalt find them no more at all.*

"AND THE FRUITS THAT THY SOUL LUSTED AFTER ARE DEPARTED FROM THEE"

The world as we know it is coming to an end. The age of wars and rumors of wars is upon us. Therefore, what does it profit a man if he gain the whole world and yet lose his own soul? All the money, prestige, and power cannot and will not save you from the judgment that is coming.

Revelation 18:17 *For in one hour so great riches is come to nought. And every shipmaster, and all the company in ships, and sailors, and as many as trade by sea, stood afar off,*

"FOR IN ONE HOUR SO GREAT RICHES IS COME TO NOUGHT"

There will come a day when all that is of value will have no value at all. For what does it profit a man if he gain the whole world but lose his own soul? For those that remain on this earth, the only thing of any value will be life itself. All the wealth and fame a man will strive to achieve will be consumed in flames in but an hour

---

Revelation 19:1 *And after these things I heard a great voice of much people in heaven, saying, Alleluia; Salvation, and glory, and honour, and power, unto the Lord our God:*

"AND AFTER THESE THINGS I HEARD A GREAT VOICE OF MUCH PEOPLE IN HEAVEN"

There are two cries that are heard. One, in the previous chapter, can be heard throughout the earth. It is a cry of anguish and pain. They are cries of cursing and loss. The sound ringing through the halls of Heaven is different, for it is filled with celebration and joy. As the earth burns, all of Heaven proclaims, "Alleluia; Salvation, and glory, and honor, and power, unto the Lord our God."

Revelation 19:16 *And he hath on his vesture and on his thigh a name written, KING OF KINGS, AND LORD OF LORDS.*

"KING OF KINGS, AND LORD OF LORDS"

If there is any comfort to be taken in this vile and messed up world, it is simply this: HE IS KING OF KINGS AND LORD OF LORDS! You can defy Him only so long, for a day of reckoning is coming! The songwriter wrote, "The king is coming, the king is coming, I just heard the trumpet sounding, and now His face I see!"

Revelation 22:12 *And, behold, I come quickly; and my reward is with me, to give every man according as his work shall be.* **13** *I am Alpha and Omega, the beginning and the end, the first and the last.*

"AND, BEHOLD, I COME QUICKLY!"

Let us approach each day as if it were our last! Have you made your preparations to meet our Lord? See! He's coming! Are you ready?

Page Index

235

243

TOPICAL INDEX

www.ingramcontent.com/pod-product-compliance
Lightning Source LLC
La Vergne TN
LVHW051113080426
835510LV00018B/2013